Out of the Shadows

Interpretations

This series provides clearly written and up-to-date introductions to recent theories and critical practices in the humanities and social sciences.

General Editor
Ken Ruthven (University of Melbourne)

Advisory Board
Tony Bennett (Griffith University)
Penny Boumelha (University of Adelaide)
John Frow (University of Queensland)
Sneja Gunew (University of British Columbia, Vancouver)
Robert Hodge (University of Western Sydney)
Terry Threadgold (Monash University)

In preparation:
Queer Theory, by Annamarie Jagose

Out of the Shadows

Contemporary German Feminism

Silke Beinssen-Hesse and Kate Rigby

MELBOURNE UNIVERSITY PRESS
1996

HQ
1623
B45
1996

Melbourne University Press
PO Box 278, Carlton South, Victoria 3053, Australia

First published 1996

Designed by Mark Davis/text-art
Typeset by Melbourne University Press in 10.5/13 pt Garamond
Printed in Malaysia by SRM Production Services Sdn Bhd

ISSN 1039-6128

National Library of Australia Cataloguing-in-Publication entry

Beinssen-Hesse, Silke, 1936– .
  Out of the shadows: contemporary German feminism.
  Bibliography.
  Includes index.
  ISBN 0 522 84592 4.

  1. Feminism—Germany. 2. Feminist theory—Germany.
  I. Rigby, Catherine, 1960– . II. Title. (Series: Interpretations).
305.420943

Contents

Contents

Preface

'German feminist theory . . . is there such a thing?' This common response, encountered not only in Australia but also in Germany, indicates the extent to which German feminist thinking has been overshadowed by French and Anglo-American feminisms. Its low profile in the English-speaking world is related above all to the paucity of translated material. The reasons for the relative 'invisibility' of German feminist theory in the German region itself are more complex. In part, this is a legacy of widespread hostility in the German women's movement to abstraction as 'typically male' and a suspicion of 'Theory' in the upper echelons of German universities in the 1970s as subversively leftist. This meant that feminist thinking in the German region has tended to be pre-sented as 'women's research' (*Frauenforschung*) on specific areas —often with an empirical orientation—rather than explicitly as a new way of analysing culture and society, even though often that was what it involved. The inability of German-speaking feminists to see how their own thinking differs from that of English- or French-speaking feminists, many of whom have doubtless had a decisive impact in the German region, also points to the universal difficulty of perceiving what one takes for granted. From the outside, it is more readily apparent that German feminist debates have been conditioned by habits of thought and recurrent themes arising from intellectual traditions and historical circumstances peculiar to the German region. In writing this introductory study, we have thus been able to turn the 'tyranny of distance' to advantage.

Rigorously selecting from the now vast amount of writing by German-speaking feminists, we have concentrated on material that is both theoretical in orientation and in some sense characteristic of German feminist thought. Nevertheless, we have endeavoured to cover a lot of ground, both geographically and intellectually. Most of the work that we refer to is by feminists in what was West Germany, but we also include material published in the former German Democratic Republic (GDR), Switzerland and Austria. It has not always been possible either to make this explicit or to discuss possible differences in orientation and approach within the German-speaking region. On the other hand, we do draw attention to such differences as they relate to disciplinary background, methodology and ideological affiliation, allowing the polyphony of German feminist voices to be heard within the confines of our own reconstruction of the debates. Moreover, respecting the characteristically strong emphasis in German feminism on the necessary connection between theory and praxis, we indicate how particular ways of thinking and modes of analysis are related to feminist politics in the wider context of the second-wave women's movement, above all in the Federal Republic of Germany (FRG).

German feminist thinking has been articulated in the shadow not only of the internationally dominant francophone and anglophone variants of feminist knowledge, but also of Germany's fascist past. Indeed, the felt necessity of confronting this past has contributed to what is in our view one of the strengths of German feminist theory, namely its characteristically historical and sociological perspective and concomitant stress on the importance of understanding the origins of one's ideas and taking responsibility for their political implications.

Two further strengths of German feminism that have conditioned our account are its interdisciplinarity, and the absence of intellectual 'superstars'. We have thus organised our presentation thematically rather than according to discipline or around key individuals, although certain names do recur. We have sought to reflect the democratic nature of German feminist debate, which has enabled the voices of younger women, freelance publicists and practising artists and film-makers to be heard alongside those of older women in positions of privilege in academia (of whom until recently there have been very few). Finally, rather than presenting our account as a linear narrative in a single impersonal voice, we have written all chapters, except the last, individually, as discrete, yet interconnected essays: Chapters 1, 4, 5 and 6 were penned by Kate, and Chapters 2, 3 and 7 by Silke. We feel that this approach is more in keeping with the feminist critique of 'objective' knowledge, since it does not efface those differences in style and in the position from which each of us speaks that have enriched our collaboration.

We would like to thank David Roberts for suggesting that we write this book for Melbourne University Press and for reading sundry drafts; Monash University for financing Silke's study leave in Germany in the planning stage of the book; the Humboldt Foundation for its generous assistance in facilitating Kate's research trip to Germany; the staff and students in the Women's Studies section of *Fachbereich* 3 at the University of Paderborn, especially Gisela Ecker and her valiant assistants, Monika Nienaber and Karin Windt, and colleagues, Maria Kublitz-Kramer and (for ergonomic assistance) Helga Grubitzsch; all those who agreed to be interviewed and gave us bibliographical assistance, notably Christina von Braun, Dorothea Dornhof, Kristin Herzog, Gudrun-Axeli Knapp, Hannelore Mabry, Elisabeth Moltmann-Wendel, Ursula Nienhaus, Irene Nierhaus, Irit Rogoff, Renate Schlesier, Walter Veit and Sigrid Weigel; the Women's Archive in Berlin (FFBIZ); Philip Thomson for his support as our Head of Department at Monash University; Dirk Diekniete and Monty Wilkinson for patiently sorting out our computing problems; Ken Ruthven and Susan Keogh for painstaking reading and extensive editorial assistance; and, last but not least, our families for their support and forbearance.

1

The Dialectic of Enlightenment

The revolution has not taken place

> But when the cry rose and was heard once more,
> 'Freedom for all!' had a mocking tone;
> For in these revolutionary storms
> It was intended to free men alone.
> No matter that yoke upon yoke was lifted
> And throne upon throne fell to dust,
> This latest struggle was for men's rights only;
> The law for women would remain unjust.
> (Luise Otto-Peters, 1986, my trans.)

The first stanza of Luise Otto-Peters' ode to revolution, 'Für Alle', was published in 1847, just before a new wave of uprisings throughout western and central Europe. It expresses the widespread disappointment and frustration felt by early feminists, who perceived that the emancipatory ideals of the Enlightenment and French Revolution had not been realised for women; even worse, that the fraternity of *citoyens* had won their freedom at the expense of that of their sisters-in-arms (Rothe, 1990). The true liberation or (in the religious register of the ecstatic final stanza of her poem) 'redemption' of men and women alike, Otto-Peters avers, will nevertheless surely come about one day. It has yet to happen, of course, despite the achievement of certain legal and

civil rights by the first-wave women's movement, despite im-
provements in women's access to higher education and paid
employment since World War II, and despite changes in social
attitudes and practices generated by second-wave feminism since
the 1970s. Indeed, two hundred years after the French Revolution,
the editors of a collection of bicentennial essays by German
feminist philosophers registered in the title of the book their sad
conclusion that 'the Revolution has not taken place' (Deuber-
Mankowsky et al., 1989). Nor have the subsequent revolutionary
upheavals in eastern Europe brought any substantial improvement
in the situation of women. On the contrary, the formerly East
German feminist contributors to a volume entitled *Gute Nacht, du
Schöne* (Mudry, 1991), believe that in some respects their situation
has declined even more dramatically than that of most men in the
region (see also Beyer, 1992; Schaeffer-Hegel, 1992). While
doubtless benefiting from the new freedoms of movement and
speech and opportunities for political participation in the greater
Federal Republic, women in eastern Germany are at present
facing high rates of unemployment, drastically reduced child-care
facilities, and a bombardment of images of the sex-objects they
are now apparently expected to become—images of 'imagined
femininity' (Bovenschen, 1979), which twenty years of western
feminist critique have done little to dislodge.

If a single theme unites the diverse thinking of German feminist
theorists—cutting across disciplinary boundaries, methodological
approaches and ideological affiliations—it is this: where do women
stand in relation to the ideals of the Enlightenment, and what
have those processes of socio-economic and political change
associated with the French Revolution meant for women? Did the
position of women gradually improve or decline with the
emergence of bourgeois society? Can the project of women's
emancipation be seen as a legitimate offspring of the bourgeois
Enlightenment, despite the fact that most eighteenth-century philosophers and politicians emphatically disowned it? Or does the
realisation of feminist aspirations not entail the end of bourgeois
(or more generally, industrial) society and its dominant values?
Can and should the ideals of 'freedom, equality and fraternity' be
appropriated by women? Have women been discriminated against

because historically these ideals have been realised only partially in particular socio-political contexts? Or are these ideals themselves inappropriate for the articulation of women's needs, interests and visions? What are these needs, interests and visions? These wide-ranging questions will recur throughout the book. I begin here with a number of distinctively German feminist perspectives on the ambivalent legacy of the Enlightenment, and more generally, on the 'dialectic of enlightenment' within both patriarchal civilisation and the feminist project itself.

The dialectic of patriarchal enlightenment: the theoretical model

A distinctive and valuable feature of much German feminist writing about enlightenment and modernity is its critical engagement with the theoretical postulates of the Frankfurt School. The history and theories of the Frankfurt School are discussed in detail by Martin Jay (1973) and Rolf Wiggershaus (1994), and the essays in Wilson and Holub (1993) exemplify a range of contemporary approaches to the dialectic of enlightenment. Founded in 1923 as an Institute of Social Research, and having a Marxist orientation, the Frankfurt School is associated above all with the philosophy and social theory of Max Horkheimer, Theodor Adorno, Herbert Marcuse and (although he was never formally a member) Walter Benjamin. Its most prominent contemporary heir is Jürgen Habermas. Rediscovered during the student movement of the late 1960s, from which West German feminism largely emerged, the work of the Frankfurt School was greeted enthusiastically by this new generation as a 'home-grown' model of radical social and cultural critique, which could not only be enlisted in the process of 'coming to terms' with the Nazi past, but also provide new perspectives on the present. 'Critical Theory', as the mode of enquiry developed by the Frankfurt School is termed, transgresses the disciplinary boundaries between philosophy and sociology, history and psychology, aesthetics and economics. It has thus informed German feminist research (which is itself generally interdisciplinary) in many areas, and shaped the reception of both feminist writing in English and (more recently) French philosophy and social theory. As a research methodology, Critical Theory will be discussed in greater detail in Chapter 8. Here, I would like to focus on the notion of the 'dialectic of enlightenment' and the critique of 'instrumental reason' (*Vernunftkritik*). Although German-speaking feminists do not always draw explicitly on the Frankfurt School, these concepts are generally taken for granted in German feminist theory, and contribute significantly to its distinctive emphases and preoccupations.

The classical formulation of the concept of a 'dialectic of enlightenment' occurs in the highly influential text of this name by Adorno and Horkheimer (1989). First published in 1944 when they were both living in exile in Los Angeles—for as socialists and Jews they were doubly at risk in Nazi Germany—this collection of essays, aphorisms and fragments is a bleak rejoinder to the optimism of nineteenth-century philosophies of history, most notably those of Hegel and Marx, for whom 'dialectical development' signified the march of human progress. For Hegel, the antagonism of ideas—the interplay of moral and intellectual 'theses' and 'antitheses' in producing ever new syntheses—facilitated the progressive self-realisation of abstract Mind or Reason in history. This process, he believed, had reached its textual culmination in his own philosophy, and its socio-political completion in the reformed Prussian state. But, according to Marx's 'materialist' corrective to Hegel's 'idealist' conception of the historical dialectic, what gave rise to new forms of social organisation and cultural expression was the antagonism of classes, defined by their relationship to the means of production. From this perspective, history was still a going concern, and would end only with the emancipation of everybody through the collective ownership of the means of production in communism.

For Adorno and Horkheimer, by contrast, 'dialectical development' meant historical regression and cultural decline. They were disillusioned with the outcome of the Bolsheviks' attempt to put Marxist theory (as reformulated by Lenin and bastardised by Stalin) into practice. They also despaired of the revolutionary potential of the working class, which had either collapsed in the face of fascist terror or been neutralised by the *promesse de bonheur* (promise of happiness) proffered by the culture industry.

4

Consequently, Adorno and Horkheimer could not share Marx's confidence in the realisability of the communist utopia. Although they draw heavily on both Hegelian and Marxian thought, their narrative about modernity has greater affinity with those sombre accounts of western civilisation to be found in Nietzsche, Freud and Weber. For this is the story neither of the triumphant self-unfolding of Reason nor of the emancipation of the masses, but of self-alienation and mass deception under the destructive dominion of a purely instrumental form of rationality.

The project of 'enlightenment', the internal dialectic of which Adorno and Horkheimer disclose, can be traced back to Ancient Greece, but assumes its modern guise only with the scientific revolution of the seventeenth century. The experimental method of empirical research proposed by Francis Bacon, and René Descartes's subjective rationalism, are seen as the main vehicles of what Weber had termed the 'disenchantment (*Entzauberung*) of nature'. By this he meant the progressive eradication of animist beliefs, the banishment of God to a distant place of origin outside His Creation, and the reduction of nature to the status of both a mathematically predictable machine and a resource to be freely exploited in the interests of capitalist economic growth. Paradoxically, Adorno and Horkheimer claim this process of 'de-mythologisation' (*Entmythologisierung*) was itself driven by a mythic fear of nature, and a concomitant desire to become free of its unpredictable onslaughts by gaining knowledge of (and therefore control over) its inner workings. They were not in a position either to see the devastating ecological consequences of this fearful and self-defeating endeavour, or to know that the *Dialectic of Enlightenment* would thereby acquire a new relevance among ecologically concerned feminists in the 1980s and 1990s (e.g. Beer, 1987b; Konnertz, 1989; Kulke and Scheich, 1992). Adorno and Horkheimer were concerned primarily with the psychosocial and political rather than the ecological implications of the project of enlightenment. They argued that although scientific positivism had itself become a dominant ideology—a modern myth of the reducibility of all phenomena to the mute facticity of numbers and the 'manipulability' (*Machbarkeit*) of the machine—it had succeeded neither in banishing the fear of nature nor enhancing human freedom; if anything, the reverse was the case. The constitution of the rational and self-determining subject as the privileged locus of knowledge and authority had certainly proved effective against traditional forms of religious and political domination. Yet the process of enlightenment had also brought new kinds of repression and oppression, both psychological and social. In seeking to emancipate himself from nature, enlightened western man had also sought to gain control over his own 'inner nature', his bodily drives and desires. Man's fear of the 'return of the repressed' increased proportionately as 'outer nature' was brought under the control of the instrumental reason of science and technology. Society's symbolic, psychological and even physical aggression towards those seen as representing this danger had likewise increased. Enlightenment had thus generated its own Other. Cast in the image of an alienated nature denied in the transcendental and unified Self, the Other has been figured variously as the savage, the homosexual, the Jew and, of course, Woman. On a social level too, scientific and technological progress made possible new forms of repression as the industrial labour force was rendered docile by the ideological opiates doled out, not by the Church, as still in Marx's day, but rather—and in Adorno's and Horkheimer's view, far more effectively—by the mass media of fascist propaganda and the culture industry.

That 'chaste and lawful marriage between the mind of man and the nature of things' proclaimed by Bacon (the *paterfamilias* of modern science) was always, as Adorno and Horkheimer observe, patriarchal in conception. Yet their own narrative of the pursuit of self-determination at the price of self-alienation and societal domination is very much a philosophy of history from a male perspective. Women appear in it primarily as embodiments of mythical Woman, that 'enigmatic image of irresistibility and powerlessness' (Adorno and Horkheimer, 1989:72) which is the focus of male fear and fascination. The *Dialectic of Enlightenment* has proved a useful point of departure in German feminist discussions of how such privileged concepts as 'reason' and 'autonomy' have been constructed historically in opposition to those of Nature and Woman. However, as feminist theorists point out (Beer, 1988; Scheich, 1988; Kulke, 1989; Schulz, 1992), Adorno and Horkheimer themselves remain trapped within the binary logic that they criticise, since their analysis still leaves women (and nature) in the position of the imaginary Other of enlightenment. Recent reflections by Kulke and Scheich (1992) on the 'dialectic of enlightenment from the perspective of women' draw attention to connections not only between 'imagined femininity' and the sexual division of labour in industrial society but also between the domination of nature and the domestic confinement of women. Such connections were either not noticed or theorised inadequately by Adorno and Horkheimer. In addition, feminists have sought to overcome the pessimistic conclusions of the *Dialectic of Enlightenment* by uncovering possibilities of resistance and transformation for women.

The view from the other side

The witch

The first major contribution to the feminist reconstruction of the dialectic of enlightenment was Silvia Bovenschen's 1978 essay on 'The Contemporary Witch, the Historical Witch and the Witch Myth'. First published in German in 1977, this is a feminist application of Critical Theory to a subject which is relatively peripheral to the work of the Frankfurt School, but becomes central when the dialectic of enlightenment is viewed from the perspective of women. In analysing the witch-hunts, Bovenschen discloses a new dimension to Adorno and Horkheimer's perception that the domination of nature entails social domination. For the violent subjugation of women as witches was instituted to curb their supposed ability to defy the 'laws' upon which the new order of the rational penetration and technical exploitation of nature depended. While the witch-hunts were crucial in order to emancipate science from the magical, mimetic relationship to nature from which it had emerged, the Church (which was itself to suffer when science became the dominant world-view of modernity) acted 'as executioner in the literal sense of the word' (Bovenschen, 1978:105). In eradicating all traces of animist magic as practised by lay people, especially women, the Church shored up its own power by claiming a monopoly on miracle. While traditionally female forms of the 'appropriation of nature' were being demonised and suppressed, women were denied access to the new scientific knowledge of nature's laws. 'Woman' thus became defined as a 'component of exploited nature'; and 'men's fear of nature's revenge was centred on her, as was their longing for harmony and reconciliation with nature' (ibid.:106), as Adorno and Horkheimer had earlier recognised.

Bovenschen also considers how some elements of the women's movement have reappropriated the figure of the witch as a symbol of female resistance. Acknowledging that 'because of their exclusion from important sectors of domination and production, [and] because of their specific social function, women ... have maintained behavioural possibilities which resist instrumental rationality', Bovenschen thinks that to this extent they 'will remain witches for as long as their oppression endures' (ibid.:119). In wanting to contain the 'contemporary witch' to the moment of resistance, Bovenschen clearly shares Adorno and Horkheimer's view of history as a 'one-way street'. Unlike some of the theorists discussed below, Bovenschen does not appear to believe in the possibility of reclaiming from the past suppressed modes of thinking and acting. In their self-definition as witches, she warns, feminist groups are in danger of replicating the imagined femininity of the patriarchal witch myth, which had hitherto perpetuated the social marginalisation and disempowerment of women.

The housewife

As indicated already, the feminist critique of enlightenment focuses on what is perceived as the major blindspot in both classical Critical Theory and that Marxist philosophy of history from which the Frankfurt School took its point of departure: namely, how the construction of Woman as the Other of reason is connected with the sexual division of labour in industrial society.

The first significant treatment of this subject in German dates from the mid 1970s. It is best exemplified in the articles of Karin Hausen (1981), Gisela Bock and Barbara Duden (1976; Duden, 1977) which are still frequently cited in contemporary feminist writing. The work of these historians was important in challenging the then common assumption that the bourgeois Enlightenment laid the foundation for the emancipation of women. They show how the abstract universalism of the *philosophes* foundered on the concrete particulars of the emergent bourgeois order. More specifically, they suggest that the sexual division of labour which emerged concurrently with the relocation of work—now defined pre-eminently as a money-earning activity outside the home—led to a decline in the social status of women. In the stratified society of premodern Europe, the identity of both men and women was defined by social position or caste, and, within the productive household or *oikos*, by status and duties. Since no farm or household business could survive without the labour of women, their work was regarded as no less essential than that of men. This changed with the dissolution of the 'whole household' and the emergence of the nuclear family, whose primary function was as a child-rearing unit, and, increasingly, basic unit of private consumption. In the middle echelons of society especially, women became economically dependent upon their money-earning menfolk. At the same time, female identity was increasingly associated with female biology, defined in terms of a specific 'nature', internal and common to all women, produced by their physiology and manifest specifically in their child-bearing capacity. Male identity, on the other hand, became increasingly contingent from the late eighteenth century, being determined less by the accident of birth than by the opportunities grasped by the individual in fashioning himself as a 'social being'. Full self-determination could only be won in that public sphere from which women were largely excluded. Those social changes which enabled men to proclaim the enlightenment project thus gave rise to a new form of female oppression, which was all the more insidious by being internalised. The over-identification of women with their sexual and reproductive function—previously assumed to be a legacy of premodern patriarchy—could now be recognised as an effect of bourgeois modernity.

In their contribution to the 1976 Summer University for women in Berlin, Bock and Duden show how this actual degradation of women was masked ideologically as idealisation. Confinement to the domestic sphere and exclusion from paid labour were glorified as a fulfilment of woman's higher nature, the fulcrum of which was deemed to be selfless love. This sentimentalisation and aestheticisation of women's domestic work is analysed further by Duden (1977). Discussing female stereotypes in the writings of Kant, Schiller and Fichte, she traces the development of the bourgeois ideal of Woman. Whereas for Kant (whose understanding is still shaped by the old order of the *oikos*) Woman figures as a lusty combatant in the marital 'battle of the sexes', she becomes with Schiller the 'beautiful soul' (*schöne Seele*) whose emotions and reason are so harmonised that her very instincts seem to be virtuous, and finally, with Fichte, the fully domesticated wife and mother, who realises herself, paradoxically, in total self-renunciation.

As a paragon of selfless devotion to husband and children, Woman was placed at the centre of the bourgeois familial sphere. No longer recognised as a productive unit, the home acquired a new compensatory significance as a place of refuge from the outside world, where 'traditional' values might be preserved from the prevailing instrumental rationality of politics and production. There the businessman or professional might recover his essential personhood and abandon himself to the pleasures of being— albeit in preparation for the necessity of doing. Longings which found no outlet in the reified 'outside world' thus tended to be channelled back into this supposedly sheltered realm of private felicity. As the embodiment of this seemingly timeless realm, Woman became the symbolic bearer of utopian hopes and was thus placed outside history and society.

Much more has been written subsequently on the imaginary woman of bourgeois modernity. In the process, the central theses of Hausen, Bock and Duden have been extended, refined, and challenged. Some feminists have radicalised their critical re-assessment of modernity, as in the theory of 'housewifisation' (*Hausfrauisierung*) developed by the sociologists and anthropologists Maria Mies, Claudia von Werlhof and Veronika Bennholdt-Thomsen (1988), which draws a connection between the historical experience of western women and that of colonised peoples. Others, such as the historian Brita Rang (1986), question Hausen's assumption of a direct link between the emergence of the bourgeois family and the polarisation of gender identity. According to Rang, what really changed in the eighteenth century was the extent to which traditional views on women were open to contestation: this prompted the need to find new ways of grounding the alleged differences between the sexes and legitimating female subordination. German feminist philosophers point out that the anti-emancipatory view of 'Woman's nature', which eventually came to serve this function, was neither universal nor intrinsic to the philosophical postulates of the Enlightenment, and they differ in their assessment of the dominant construction of woman as the 'moral sex'. Did this constitute an immanent critique of instrumental reason, as Steinbrügge (1987, 1989) has argued with regard to Rousseau? Or was it simply the necessary counterpart of the political discourse of 'human rights' (which by implication applied only to propertied men in the public sphere) as Schaeffer-Hegel (1989) maintains? A further question concerns the extent to which women really were as confined to the home as the new ideologies of 'women's place' implied. Throughout the nineteenth century, middle-class women were active in charitable work and neighbourhood networks, while lower class women often had little option but to participate in industrial labour. The discursive association of women with the private sphere nonetheless ensured that their voluntary and even paid employment was interpreted, as far as possible, according to the code of domesticity. Similarly, the labour associated with home has continued to be seen, until recently, as women's responsibility, while remaining invisible as 'work' (Schissler, 1990).

Despite differences in orientation and interpretation, German feminist discussions of imagined femininity commonly emphasise the historicity (rather than the universality) of the polarisation of gender difference. This is also true of Sigrid Weigel's article (1987b) on Woman as the 'stranger at home', which locates the modern mythologisation of femininity within the dialectic of enlightenment. Weigel's work is interesting methodologically in its mediation of Critical Theory and French post-structuralism. Her subject is the cultural construction of Woman in relation to 'the Savage' within what she calls—following Foucault (1972)— the 'discourse' of enlightenment. Linked metonymically by their discursive location as the Other of reason, Woman and Savage join those other Others (such as myth and magic, dream and madness, childhood and the body) discussed by Böhme and Böhme (1985) in their influential study of Kant. Weigel, however, thinks that these terms should not be conflated. Analysing philosophical texts by Rousseau and Diderot in the context of eighteenth-century travel literature, she shows that while the Savage stands in a teleological relationship to civilisation as a 'primitive stage' Europeans have surpassed, Woman stands in a moral-intellectual relationship to 'man', who assumes the superior position of enlightened rationality *vis-à-vis* her predominantly emotional 'feminine nature'. However, as the period of discovery draws to a close, it is this 'close stranger' (*nahe Fremde*) who emerges finally as the primary Other within the self-understanding of enlightenment, to which the other terms now tend to become assimilated.

Weigel reads the conceptualisation of female sexual identity in such terms as innocence, modesty, grace and virtue (as studied by Bock, Duden and Hausen) as a projection of the enlightenment ideal of a harmonious, humanised nature. This dream of domesticated nature, however, has as its counterpart in the dialectic of enlightenment the nightmare of regression. The 'white gown of innocence' adorning the late eighteenth-century projections of the feminine is 'always threatening to tear apart' and reveal what centuries of witch-burning had sought to suppress: Woman as the avatar of another, 'wild' nature, the feared object of new strategies of domination and control (Weigel, 1987b:180).

The hysteric

Towards the end of the nineteenth-century, the feminine Other of reason assumed a new guise in the figure of the hysteric. In the classical Freudian analysis of hysteria, this condition is a pathological response to the libidinal repressions required of the bourgeois 'angel in the home'. More significantly, according to Christina von Braun (1985), hysteria is symptomatic of the wider pathology of western civilisation. Her lengthy work, entitled *Nicht Ich*, remains one of the most original and provocative recastings by German feminists of the dialectic of enlightenment. Her approach is informed both by Critical Theory and by certain theories of 'postmodernity', developed largely in Paris, where she herself lived from 1969 to 1981. For von Braun seeks to theorise not only the *domination* of nature, but also its *displacement* by the order of the 'simulacral', as Jean Baudrillard has named the postmodern substitution of image for reality (Baudrillard, 1994). Von Braun argues that this substitution has occurred through a process of ever-increasing 'abstraction'. Originating with the creation of writing, by the twentieth century this has generated a new second-order Reality, which has totally obliterated material reality. A return to 'nature', 'the body' or 'woman' is no longer possible, as these exist only as the projections of that abstract Logos (the Word or Law), whose history von Braun traces; these images have now 'become flesh' in the simulacral world created by Logos in its own image. Unlike Baudrillard, von Braun also emphasises the resistance encountered by this process. In her view hysteria, the classic 'female disease', functioned historically as an unconscious protest by the body in its scandalous materiality against its negation by the dictates of abstract reason. Significantly, hysteria reaches its high point around 1900 as a corollary of the completion of the industrial revolution. However, now that the female body exists solely as artifice, the only possibility of resistance is to deny the fake/false/phallic (*phallschen*) Body. With Logos now made flesh, asceticism emerges as a strategy of 'disincarnation'—a refusal to make oneself available for 'consumption'. Thus anorexia nervosa has replaced hysteria as the key form of protest against the dominion of Logos. By the same logic, writing (once the means by which the Logos unfolded itself) now acquires a new value. For while the writing of the past retains memories of the war against embodied reality, writing in the present becomes subversive to the extent that it refuses to mirror (and therefore endorse) the reality of the new Reality. Ironically, von Braun is herself a film-director and thus finds herself endeavouring to counter that simulacral world of the image which her own favoured medium has helped to bring about.

In her grand theory of civilisation as the elimination of difference—a theme she pursues further in a more recent collection of essays on history (1989)—there is no room either for utopian visions or programmes of social change. For by operating according to the same ratiocentric and bureaucratic logic, these have always promoted the cause of Logos. As Christine Kulke observes, von Braun's pessimistic conclusions derive in part from her failure to distinguish the abstractions of Logos from what Adorno and Horkheimer sometimes refer to as the 'mimetic' dimension of reason: a non-instrumental and non-imperialistic way of making sense of and interacting with the world, the recovery of which might enable us to get beyond the dialectic of enlightenment (Kulke, 1989:104). Like Baudrillard's theory of simulation, von Braun's theory of abstraction tends to mask the fact that the simulacral Reality produced by the Logos could not exist without the material reality it has apparently displaced. If nature and the body had been wholly eliminated by Nature and the Body, there would be no civilisation left to critique. In so far as the conquest of the body is necessarily continuous with the cultural construction of the Body, anorexia is a highly ambivalent strategy of resistance. It may not always be easy or even possible to tell where one ends and the other begins. But any woman who refuses to conform to the *phallsch* image of femininity by 'parodying' it—transforming sexily slim into asexually emaciated— will also injure, if not destroy, her material base in the process.

Double-bind: the dialectic of feminist enlightenment

Feminism is an 'untimely' phenomenon in being marked by what the German philosopher Ernst Bloch calls the 'simultaneity of the non-simultaneous' (1977)—the coexistence, that is, of ideologies (or in post-structuralist parlance, discourses) pertaining to different historical moments. Moreover, second-wave feminists began to lay claim to the emancipatory inheritance of the Enlightenment just at a time when its dark side was becoming increasingly difficult to overlook. When feminism re-emerged as a mass social movement in the early 1970s, the problem that concerned German women was generally not so much the internal dialectic of enlightenment as the historical exclusion of women from its emancipatory project. The attempt to 'catch up' with men in this respect is now seen to have led women into a double-bind. Rejecting those attributes and roles traditionally ascribed to women *[handwritten marginal note: although gave up on methodology, haven't given up on others (contrary)]*

as an oppressive ideology from which they wished to liberate themselves, feminists generally ended up modelling their emancipation on 'masculine' norms of self-determination and self-realisation. In entering the public sphere, women have been obliged to accommodate themselves to precisely the kind of instrumental rationality that feminists had sought to overcome, and in so doing have risked losing the socially transformative potential they derive from their different history and social position. As Christel Eckart (1992:101) observes, with the end of 'femininity' (through the individualisation of women) a potential locus of resistance appears threatened. To adopt a 'masculine' model of self-determination as a means of emancipation from the body now appears too high a price for women to pay. Whereas men have been able to see this in terms of the subjugation of the Other, for women, this Other is 'their own': '*mater/materia* (mother/material) which has to be mastered and rationalised first and foremost in the struggle for self-preservation, the woman's body, the *skandalon* of a rationally orientated history' (Weigel, 1990b:110). The dominant ideal of autonomy may well entail for women a form of self-alienation even more profound than that hitherto experienced by men. On the other hand, many German feminist theorists share Sigrid Weigel's view that the refusal of enlightenment and history—'exemplified by a return to a supposedly happier (matriarchal) pre-history' (ibid.:120)—is equally unacceptable, as this response evades the complexity of women's position as both victim and participant, however marginalised, subordinate or invisible, in patriarchal civilisation.

In Walter Benjamin's ninth 'Thesis on the Philosophy of History' Weigel finds a 'dialectical image' which, when read by a woman, conveys something of this complexity. Benjamin describes history as an 'angel' whose 'face is turned towards the past', and who would willingly repair the damage he sees if only he were not propelled into the future by the 'storm' that 'we call progress' (Benjamin, 1973:259f.). According to Weigel, the problem for women is to find a perspective from which our gaze is usurped neither by the angel who sees civilisation as catastrophe nor by Benjamin's consensual 'we', for whom the same process signifies 'progress'.

Yet the desire to identify with the angel—and return to myths of 'wholeness' in the midst of a still relatively new project of feminist enlightenment—is perhaps itself a response to the double-bind produced by women's attempts to 'catch up'. Evidence for such a dialectic of feminist enlightenment might be found, for example, in the reassessment of motherhood, which has been particularly radical in Germany. No doubt partly in reaction against the excesses of the Nazi idealisation and manipulation of motherhood, German feminists in the 1970s were generally enthusiastic recipients of Shulamith Firestone's techno-socialist vision of self-determination via emancipation from the womb (1970). Today, however, German feminists are almost universally suspicious of the new reproductive technologies, which are seen as appropriating women's exclusive ability to create new human life and negating an important aspect of female sexuality. Again, the Nazi experience is frequently drawn upon, but now as highlighting the dangers of eugenics (e.g. Mies, 1992).

A general perception that the modernist concept of emancipation makes women vulnerable to new forms of instrumentalisation and domination has resulted in a positive reassessment of the status of women in premodern European and non-western societies. In some cases, traditionally feminine functions and attributes have been reaffirmed. This connection is explored by Cornelia Klinger (1986), who is generally critical of what she calls 'traditionalist' or 'romantic' conceptions of women's emancipation. Klinger recognises the serious problems that have given rise to this 'backward-looking' model of emancipation, which is paralleled by reassertions of a supposedly premodern cultural identity in post-colonial conditions. But she argues that this approach gets us nowhere, since it merely reverses the binary dualisms that characterise the dominant discourse of western civilisation. Similar criticisms have been levelled at postmodernist celebrations of femininity, such as that of Hassauer and Roos (1988). In their view, enlightenment concepts and practices are hopelessly compromised and totally inadequate for dealing with the disastrous situation engendered by the illusion of 'universal knowledge and universal control'. Thus, 'the future is not enlightenment', they proclaim, 'the future is femininity' (ibid.:47). What 'femininity' might mean in practice is intentionally not defined here, but it is clearly situated, as in Adorno and Horkheimer, on the far side of reason.

As Conrad and Konnerz (1986:10) observe, the feminist critique of instrumental reason is an interrogation of enlightenment from the position of the Other. Yet women risk remaining trapped in the dialectic by too absolute an identification with the Other. For this reason, many German feminists have rejected simple reversals of the woman-and-enlightenment dualism, favouring instead more differentiated views such as that proposed by Weigel (1990b). The real challenge for feminist theory in the 1980s, Klinger concludes, was to develop alternative models of emancipation, which avoid the pitfalls of the modernist conception of autonomy without surrendering altogether the values of self-determination and equality. This in turn required the development of new notions of female subjectivity and culture, which acknowledge difference (including differences among women) without simply reinscribing the old myth of Woman as the Other of Enlightenment.

2

Reality-engendering Myth or the Enslaved Mind

Historians of women have concentrated on four main problems, the primary one being the retrieval of facts. This is a monumental task because for millennia women's lives were considered unhistorical, unimportant and uninteresting, and were consequently left unrecorded. Since women were neither active in the public sphere nor (until quite recently) normally literate, the sources we have are rarely their versions of events. A common task for all historians of women is to find appropriate source material. Problems in this area are similar to those facing historians of the lower classes or other disadvantaged groups.

The second concern of historians of women is to confront the phenomenon of inevitable bias, given the influence of interpretation in the mediation of fact. Attempting to achieve a greater degree of openness, honesty and awareness, women historians tend to introduce themselves, speak in the first person, record their reactions and admit to the emancipatory concerns that often lead them to investigate particular areas.

An important project of feminist historians is to expose and account for masculine bias towards women, not only in the recording of history but more generally in the interpretation of women's role in culture. This has led to a new field of history which Bovenschen (1979) calls the history of the imagined woman. Since bias is composed of a variety of factors—including oversights, processes of symbolisation, and the conscious or semiconscious indoctrination of a dependent group, in order to privilege the dominant one—historians resort to various kinds of psychological, sociological and economic theories in attempting to explain it.

This opens up a fourth area of research for feminist historians, seeing that the public and cultural spokespersons for women have almost invariably been men. The few women writers and artists whose work has been recognised can be assumed not to have escaped indoctrination, and to have been subject to various pressures in a basically alien environment. The interesting question therefore is how women in other ages perceived themselves.

The imagined woman

In investigating the imagined woman, feminist historians have frequently resorted to (and often modified) theories developed by male sociologists and psychologists. Feminist thought, apparently, can be at best critical but never independent of the patriarchal tradition; this dilemma will be referred to again in Chapter 8. But let us first consider five propositions concerning the imagined woman.

- The supposed woman of history is more often than not an imagined woman.

One of the first to examine the phenomenon of the imagined woman was Silvia Bovenschen (1979), whose history of eighteenth-century literature has been very influential. She voices an early warning to those hoping to reconstruct from the wealth of literary representations of women by both male and female authors what historians have not told us about the real lives of men and women. Literary representations of women should never be thought of as revealing the lives or aspirations of real women. What they reflect (and this too is important) are the myths imposed upon real women.

- Women have been subjected at various times to indoctrination in the interests of a society that favoured the changing needs of men.

Like Karin Hausen and Barbara Duden, Bovenschen perceives myths of femininity as a form of ideology that legitimates the traditional subjection of women whenever new forms and ideas of self-determination become available for some men.

This process of indoctrination continued throughout the nineteenth century and into the twentieth. Hanna Hacker (1984) has conducted an interesting study of the meta-language of Austrian sexologists in the late nineteenth century and shown how it dominated lesbian women's perceptions of their identity. It not only silenced them and seriously affected their life-styles, but also made it virtually impossible for heterosexual women to approach their sisters, acknowledge what they had in common, and express informed opinions about their differences. Consciously or unconsciously, men perceived it to be in their interests (as a measure of damage control) to persuade lesbians that they were quasi-men to whom men's privileges were due, and quite different from 'normal' women who, in spite of their incipient rebelliousness, were still destined by nature for motherhood and domesticity.

Hacker interrogates the silences that characterise women's concerns at the intersection of lesbianism and the women's movement and at a time when middle-class women had both the education and the leisure to express themselves eloquently. Her work shows that the thematisation of silence is a productive approach to the problem of women's absences from history. If women are overwhelmed by alien definitions and images of themselves, and if the words available to them have already been co-opted for masculine purposes, inevitably they will feel deprived of their voice. Hacker's study raises important questions about the complicity of language, particularly the language of cultural institutions, in the silencing of women.

Whenever indoctrination is discussed, national socialism comes to mind. Surprisingly, however, Christine Wittrock's 1983 study of images of woman in fascism shows that these were generally traditional and to some extent contradictory. In her view, power over women was exercised in that period primarily through rulings, not symbols and ideologies.

- Infantile experiences of the primal mother can affect individuals and the cultures they influence, and give rise to images of women that have little to do with everyday realities.

History's imaginary women are approached differently by the psychoanalyst Renée Meyer zur Capellen (1993) in her work on the twelfth century, which derives theoretically from a modification of Freudian theory. In Freud's favouring of the Oedipal stage of development she sees repressions and biases in his own psyche at work. By contrast, she thinks that the most powerful cultural forces emanate from infantile experience of an originally symbiotic relationship with the primal mother as a paradisal state of profusion, which offers complete satisfaction and creates feelings of omnipotence. There is, however, a dark side to this relationship. For if the mother withdraws from her child or fails to provide satisfaction she is blamed for her absences and inadequacies. Her presence is taken for granted because she is not perceived as having a separate identity. In other words, the mother is either overlooked or seen to be hostile.

The normal child feels a strong need to be independent of the mother's unpredictability, and free of the ego-wounding sense of powerlessness associated with her absence. This drive towards independence also characterises stable periods of history. But in periods of considerable social change, when identity is under threat, narcissistic defence mechanisms tend to be set in motion: the primal mother as ideal object may be projected for example on to man or woman as lovers, on to one's social group, country, status or god. This results in a tendency towards internalisation and the abnormal development of fantasies that can be both regressive and progressive. In regressive fantasies the mother and her symbolic representatives are seen as inaccessible or available only in a visionary form; as such they require renunciation. In progressive fantasies, on the other hand, feelings of omnipotence allow people to challenge social institutions.

Looking at the troubadour tradition, Meyer zur Capellen concludes that songs in praise of women had nothing to do with the real women of the time, who were generally treated badly. Then why did the exponents of violence, the knights, develop this new conception of love? In this period, she explains, the feudal knights were losing power to a new central government, determined to control their belligerence. At the court of William of Aquitaine, where the troubadour tradition first developed, loss of power and prestige resulted in a narcissistic wounding which led to regressive fantasies by analogy with the primary object, the imagined mother. In infantile experience, dependency can be fantasised without narcissistic injury or shaming; better still, the fantasised object (the woman who symbolises the primal mother) proves to be controllable. Meyer zur Capellen characterises troubadour love as a 'transitional' ideal, not unlike those 'transitional objects' (teddy bears and the like) described by the prominent American psychologist D. W. Winnicott, which mediate between ourselves and the world. She produces detailed evidence that the troubadour love ideal prevailed in southern and northern France (as well as in Germany) for only limited periods that coincided with crucial times of adjustment. Well aware that their protests against subjugation would be useless, the knights had to sublimate their anger. Thus they invented the ideal woman with whose virtuous perfection (so remote from their own violent life-style) they could identify. The projection of virtue on to women allows men to continue engaging in such war-like pursuits as the crusades. But on the other hand, the ideal woman gradually assumes the role of a moderating super-ego, and facilitates the acceptance of traditionally feminine values.

Women suitably represented virtue for a number of reasons. Never having been permitted to follow their drives to the same extent as men, women as primal mothers were perceived as above all loving and caring. And because in that period love of men was legitimated only in the form of fealty, women might direct men away from heathen values to the Christian God, whose characteristics were always more feminine than knightly, and who was being promoted by an increasingly powerful Church in support of the king and his project of pacifying the land. As Meyer zur Capellen's work implies, cultural fantasies and cultural rebellions involving women may well always derive to some extent at least from infantile experiences.

- Throughout the modern period women have been both symbols and victims of men's fear of the unfamiliar or alien.

German feminist scholars in many disciplines have been more fascinated and irritated by the historical, sociological and episte-mological implications of Horkheimer's and Adorno's *Dialectic of Enlightenment* than with any other theoretical tradition. Without referring to Horkheimer and Adorno directly, Christina von Braun (1989) has recently published an impressive rival theory of post-Enlightenment European history and women's role in it.

Horkheimer and Adorno emphasise the unintended tyrannies and alienations entailed in the emancipatory project of rationally understanding, controlling and utilising nature. Their point of departure is the philosophical and technological tradition of the Enlightenment. Von Braun, however, traces the impact of moder-nity to the age of discovery, a project parallel to enlightenment. Civilisation was driven not by fear of the irrational (as Adorno and Horkheimer posit) but rather by a fear of the unknown, and the desire to acquire and domesticate anything perceived as foreign, strange, different, or other. This manifested itself in the colonisation and assimilation of foreign cultures, and led eventually to a domestication of what vestiges remained of the old cultures. Modern tourism has now reached the stage where travellers need no longer undergo the inconvenience of the unknown or the unexpected. When we travel we tend to see only what we have been shown previously or intended to see or are already informed about. Predictability and loss of novelty breed boredom; safety can also be a form of deprivation and death. Here too a dialectic of enlightenment is active; what was intended to preserve us from danger has turned out to be itself a danger.

As noted in Chapter 1, under patriarchal conditions, women are always perceived as the Other: something non-identical with that generic human being, man, and therefore something peculiar, mysterious, improper and only semi-human. This phenomenon is analysed by Simone de Beauvoir in *The Second Sex* (1953). The domestication of the unfamiliar, therefore, was always a project also directed against women. Like colonised cultures, women have been subjugated and falsified in an endeavour to obliterate their difference. Recast as man's binary opposite, Woman becomes palatable through her projected aura of the 'exotic'.

Behind the endeavour to domesticate and colonise the world, von Braun sees a narcissistic habit of mind incapable of loving anything other than its mirror image—a mentality particularly prevalent in Germany during the last two centuries. Its symptoms include the *Liebestod* syndrome of Romanticism (first developed by Novalis) where the real woman must die because in reality she is loved only as an extension of the masculine self which must eventually be internalised; the popular Romantic motif of the double; the theme of incestuous love, so prominent in late nineteenth- and early twentieth-century German literature, which also tends to require the sacrificial death of an identical sister; and the racist excesses of the Nazi period that signify a total inability to tolerate any deviation from an 'Aryan' norm with which the subject identifies. These all manifest an obsession with the familiar. So too does the increasingly widespread substitution of the imaginary woman for the real woman.

Von Braun shows that other conquests of the unfamiliar also had their inception in the age of discovery. To demonstrate this, she analyses the metamorphoses of that quintessential representative of the seventeenth century, Don Juan. In a period obsessed with the injunction to be mindful of death (*memento mori*), its inescapability seemed the last barrier to man's conquest of the world. Don Juan is in pursuit of the immortal body, first by defying God and the devil to resurrect the dead, but subsequently through the sexual conquest of women. Seen as epitomising body and materiality, women are by virtue of their sexuality the source of all earthly pleasure. While hundreds of thousands of real women were being burnt at the stake for their supposed sexual depravity, the erotic woman Don Juan yearns for was invented, and captured men's imaginations as the seductress and witch of their most thrilling dreams. The image was enduring. In the nineteenth century it found another personification in *Carmen*, but at the very time that *Carmen* was taking the stages of Europe by storm, Victorian puritanism was strait-lacing women into motherhood and erotic frigidity. The imaginary woman triumphed as the vamp, the symbol of man's desire for life and pleasure, but also the object of male symbolic violence, as Carmen's ultimately tragic end exemplifies.

Von Braun shows how boredom with a domesticated, un-mysterious and unchallenging universe leads men into ever more dangerous realms of unreality. A film-maker herself, she draws attention to the power of photography and film—both heavily implicated in giving verisimilitude to fantasies—to divest even real-life footage of its reality. She warns women, and in particular feminists, not to take as real the images of themselves that surround them and above all to reject an allegedly 'essential' femininity invented by men to satisfy their own desires.

- Imagined femininity can become a cultural interpretative model.

Most of the theories discussed so far attempt to explain historical misrepresentations of women by investigating the psychopathology of men. Such theories tend to see men as to some extent the culprits of history. Claudia Honegger (1978, 1984) distances herself from such assumptions. Instead, she is interested in the mechanisms that lead to the development and persistence of those fantasies of Woman that enable cultures to react to patterns of socio-economic change. Such patterns are too complex and far-reaching, she maintains, to permit the ascription of guilt to any single group. The fact that the victims always seem to be women can be explained only by looking in detail at the period in question.

Honegger's sophisticated essay on the witch-hunts, published in 1978, makes use of Ulrich Oevermann's theory of 'cultural interpretative models'. These are interpretations of the world that have a 'generative status', in that they generate not only attitudes and events but also a history of their own, even though this is embedded in the wider history of the period. Honegger notes the similarity between Oevermann's theory and Pierre Bourdieu's concept of the *habitus* as a 'generative grammar of models of behaviour', but is critical of Bourdieu on account of his rigidity. Oevermann's cultural interpretative models are to be understood as

historically changeable, open, constantly moving systems, that while structuring the actions and attitudes of subjects have not only generative but also assimilatory characteristics. As interpretative systems formulated in the vernacular, they resemble porous structures that internally guarantee tradition and externally 'translation' and adjustment to the real coercive forces of culture (Honegger, 1978:27, my trans.).

In the early modern period, Honegger maintains, the witch became just such an interpretative model: the witch offered explanations in a confusing period, and vouchsafed the threatened identities of people. The conditions that evoked this sense of crisis were the developing money economy and the rise of towns which housed a bourgeois class that undermined the feudal order. The Church was undergoing a crisis of legitimacy, manifest among other things in the proliferation and brutal suppression of heretical movements: this explains the genesis of delusion and dogmatism characteristic of the witch persecutions. Complementing the development and stabilisation of the interpretative model of the witch-as-evil-woman was the growing importance of the image of the Virgin Mary as the good woman. Neither image bears resemblance to the lived experience of women in this period.

In earlier centuries the phenomenon of witchcraft had been denied or played down by the Church, and treated by the secular courts as a form of assault. The publication in 1487 of the *Malleus Maleficarum* by Sprenger and Institoris inaugurated the period of persecution. A concoction of heathen folklore and custom, heretical doctrine and superstitions, it first gave definition to a belief in witchcraft as a form of power peculiar to vengeful women. While the witch-model appears to be medieval in its recourse to the supernatural, it also pre-empts modernity in its need to rationalise and to match apparently inexplicable events with causes and agents. There was a social need to persecute witches as symbolic embodiments of the dangers posed by all the inexplicable changes and threats that came in the wake of the upheavals of early modernity. That need was so strong that it overrode Christian theology and ethics as well as the far-reaching doctrinal changes brought about by the Reformation. It developed a force of its own with a complex analytical system no longer controlled by the Church or any other agency.

Such interpretative systems, therefore, have their own momentum, and are subject to both internal and external influences that allow them to adjust to the changing needs of the periods in which they are active. With a wealth of detail Honegger supports her contention that the interpretative model of the witch passed through three clearly defined stages in its two-hundred-year duration. Significantly, its eventual demise did not come as the result of an exposure of its fallaciousness; instead, the model simply became irrelevant and disappeared from every geographical region which experienced the breakthrough into modernity. Honegger, who is by training a sociologist, makes sense of a profusion of puzzling detail in a historical period full of paradoxes and oddities. Employing what was originally a sociological theory, she powerfully demonstrates the historical impact of the imaginary, which she argues is neither a philosophical theory nor a doctrine of faith but a phantasm whose operative mechanisms can be described. But her contribution to the history of imagined femininity does not explain why the symbols and victims of this phantasm are women, or why women seem to have been remembered throughout history primarily as the bearers of male imaginings.

Her implied explanations are to be found in the historical details she recounts. These include the Church's perceived need to regenerate itself by enforcing celibacy; the concomitant cult of the Virgin; the closing of convents and the exclusion of women from the Church, where they were perceived as a threat to male purity; demographic asymmetry, and the plight of superfluous women who no longer had convent retreats; the exclusion of women from trade and commerce in the wake of changed economic conditions; their consequent need to resort to devious ways of making a living; the association of women with fertility, which led to their being blamed for infertility; the prominence of disaffected women in heretical sects which initially seemed to espouse their emancipation, and the threat this posed for the traditional order of society; and later the enforced recruitment of women to work in the manufactories as the new urban proletariat.

In a more recent study Honegger (1991) examines the pseudo-scientific definition of the 'characteristics' of the sexes by physical anthropologists (and, increasingly, medical scientists) in the first half of the nineteenth century. These, she finds, constitute another cultural interpretative model in response to the complex pressures of modernity. In the second half of the eighteenth century, a range of opinion was permitted in response to those disturbing socio-economic changes that were impacting on the lives of women but, as the nineteenth century progressed, accounts of the 'nature' of women become more rigid and politically motivated. Confusingly, what is no doubt a regressive tendency for women is embedded in a progressive development for 'mankind', namely, a shift away from the body–spirit dualism of Descartes to a holistic view of 'man' as a psycho-physical entity. This new approach prompts the development of new human sciences (such as anthropology, modern medicine, psychology, ethnology and sociology) that are empirical rather than speculative. In the dialectic of enlightenment, what is productive in one respect is destructive in another: the progressive project to individuate 'man' is counteracted by the regressive typification of woman. Specific scientific methods developed in conjunction with these disciplines (including analogical thinking, the privileging of the visual, and the comparative approach) provide the tools for this new scientific definition of woman. Woman is now forever being contrasted with man and, by analogy, her reproductive organs, loose flesh, fine nerve fibres, and so on are given far-reaching interpretations. Honegger points out that the cultural interpretative model of the sexual character is still an active social force today. Horkheimer and Adorno's theory of the dialectic of enlightenment enables Honegger to achieve a critical perspective withheld in her earlier work.

In search of women's perceptions of themselves

In view of the myths, fantasies and prescriptions that have shaped the dominant images of women, it is not surprising that historians should have begun to search for 'real' ones. Bovenschen (1979) suggests that the letters of Rahel Levin-Varnhagen, for example, present something like a woman's true consciousness of herself. And elsewhere she wonders whether modern women who call themselves witches might be tapping into a genuine feminine tradition, albeit formed by the historical experience of oppression and marginalisation (Bovenschen, 1978).

By a stroke of good fortune, the historian Barbara Duden (1991a) came across material that enabled her to study how women actually perceived their bodies in the early eighteenth century. Her work is based on detailed notes by a semi-trained medical practitioner, Dr J. P. Storch, who had extraordinarily unanatomical and even health-defeating notions of the body. His notes reveal the distrust and confusion with which the women he describes viewed themselves. Whether because of men or not, they seem to have what is by our standards an unreal perception of themselves, although this apparent unreality may well be an accurate symbolic reflection of their lives.

As is almost always the case, the medical records about those women's illnesses were kept by a man. But their circumstantial features, viewed collectively, lend support to their authenticity: the meticulousness with which Storch recorded what the women apparently told him; the vast number of cases he reports; the fact that Storch's father had practised within the popular paramedical tradition; that Storch's own training had been too rudimentary to allow him to be significantly indoctrinated with the medical theories of the time; that the women were in the habit of consulting a wide variety of paramedics with very different levels and types of training; that because decorum forbade the doctor to examine his women patients physically, he had to rely exclusively on their epistolary or oral reports; and the extent of agreement among Storch's many patients about the nature of the body and its deficiencies suggest that in a period when women were normally illiterate and excluded from the professions, Storch's material is as authentic as we can hope to have at our disposal.

Duden's study could be taken further. Because we hear very little about male patients and their perceptions (also recorded by Storch) it is difficult to isolate what is specifically feminine. Nor is it easy to tell whether perceptions of the body generally may have been determined in this period by the experiences of women, who traditionally were equated with the body, but there are indications that this may have been the case.

According to Storch's female patients, a healthy body is constantly relieved by the excretion of fluids. Foremost among these are the menstrual flow and lactation, but other 'flows' can be induced by suppurating sores and rashes, by blister plasters, the procedure of bleeding, or by wounds, often made deliberately and kept open by fontanels. Analogies with menstruation and lactation seem to have overridden comfort and hygiene; even the health and survival of foetuses was often at risk from this obsession with inducing menstruation. Another characteristic of early eighteenth-century body-perception was that the fluids could move about the body randomly, so that milk that had dried up might be exuded from a rash or from the vagina.

Duden leaves her findings unadulterated by interpretation but one wonders whether the more diffuse sexuality of women could have led to such anti-anatomical perceptions. The most common cause of illness is perceived to be the 'mishap', an often quite slight change in conditions and circumstances. Again, it is interesting to speculate on whether the confined life of women and the rigidity of social structures are at work here: did men also consider themselves endangered by mishaps? The most frequent fear expressed by Storch's patients was that their bodies might stagnate: hence the importance of keeping the flows moving. Perhaps this tells us a good deal about their stagnant lives. Duden herself points out that they did not appear to be content and happy people, but were deeply suspicious of their bodies. Her comparisons with what is known of perceptions of the body in earlier periods show the importance of further research, since perceptions of the Renaissance body, the early eighteenth-century body, and the modern body differ enormously from one another.

What emerges from Duden's study is that bodily experience, which historians had considered traditionally to be the bastion of invariable nature, is just as historically determined as any other aspect of human life. Since we all tend to mythologise ourselves, her book shows us that our self-interpretation is unlikely to be independent of our patriarchal conditioning and situation. Storch's eighteenth-century patients appear to be damaged creatures who seem almost to have needed visible wounds in order to come to an understanding of themselves. In other words, discovering the authentic consciousness of women may not reveal any essence we would want to identify with. But such a discovery can help us considerably to understand our sisters who lived centuries ago. And it provides evidence of the sort of damage patriarchal society has done to women throughout history, both by imposing social restrictions on them and by focusing ideologically on Woman as body. Considerable progress could be made in the critical study of the imagined or imaginary woman if more source material of the quality of Storch's notebooks were found.

In conclusion, the importance of studying the imagined woman historically cannot be stressed too strongly, for she still haunts our lives in her different manifestations. The problem is exacerbated by the fact that both men and women in search of historical sources often turn to imaginative writing because there is so little real history available. Up to a point, of course, we are all constantly interpreting ourselves and historians are not immune to myth-making. The difference is that because women were not able to invent and record their own myths, they were largely at the mercy of those devised about them by men in response to men's needs. And since these myths were time-honoured and all pervasive, women often naively mistook them for reality, and still do. Consequently historians need to uncover both the origins and rationale of these myths, and the effects they have had on the lives of real women. At this point, the history of the imagined woman feeds back into history as the retrieval of facts, in so far as an awareness of prescriptions and imaginings is needed for a critical reading of sources. In order to retrieve biographical facts from hagiographies, for example, we need to know what the stereotypical (and presumably superimposed) prescriptions for sainthood were (see Opitz, 1984a). To free the Empress Maria Theresia from her inappropriate glorification as mother of the nation, we need to know what was expected of women at that time, and why (see Barta, 1984).

The subjection of women and their bodies to ideological misrepresentations is illuminated by the distinction made in Monika Maron's novel, *Stille Zeile Sechs* (1991), between *Leibeigenschaft* (the ownership of the body, as in serfdom or slavery) and

Geisteigenschaft (the ownership of the mind, as in ideologically governed absolute states). As Germany has been subjected twice this century to totalitarian ideological systems, first under national socialism and then communism, it is perhaps not surprising that German feminists have paid particular attention to the mental enslavement of women and its consequences.

This enslavement has probably been particularly severe in Germany during the last two centuries, given the normative influence of highly abstract thinking in philosophical idealism and physical anthropology. Prescriptions for how women should behave—common in most countries—are a form of confinement. But specifying the character and thinking of women is a form of violation, and mythologising and reinventing women can approximate to annihilation (von Braun, 1989:180; Bronfen, 1992; see also Bachmann, 1990). Unless such acts of violence are exposed, German feminists argue, the emancipation of women is unlikely to make much progress. For although each of us may live creatively by a personal myth, women are incapacitated by prescriptive and patriarchal public myths. Feminist histories of the imagined woman are intended to help women to become more perceptive and more vigilant. In this sense, we should describe such enquiries as feminist historiography rather than simply history about women.

3

Facets of Patriarchy

The historical dimension of patriarchy

While patriarchy has become one of the most commonly and passionately used terms in feminist discourse, it is by no means unambiguous. Literally, it denotes a society in which the *paterfamilias* is politically, socially and culturally dominant. Feminists often use it more loosely to refer to all sexist and male-dominated societies in which women are subordinated and largely excluded from public life. This ignores the distinction between warrior societies dominated by unattached males (of which national socialism was a recent example) and family-based patriarchies, which are very different in nature and structure and have undergone considerable changes throughout the centuries (Schaumberger and Schottroff, 1992:62–3). The known historical cultures were almost without exception male-dominated. Evidence for the existence of an original pre-patriarchal society has to be drawn, therefore, from controversial interpretations of myths and prehistoric findings that derive from preliterate periods, and analogies with ethnological studies of matrilineal or matrilocal societies. Historians, who rely on written records, are likely to produce different results from archeologists, mythologists, palaeolinguists and ethnologists. Thus the historian Gerda Lerner argues that non-patriarchal societies never existed (Lerner, 1986), while the mythologist Robert Graves is convinced they were once widespread (Graves, 1961). However, even in the case of societies organised along matrilineal and matrilocal lines and known to have worshipped female goddesses served by priestesses, it is difficult to determine the role and influence of actual women. Consequently, historians and prehistorians avoid the term 'matriarchy', which implies the rule of women (or, more precisely, mothers) and prefer to speak instead of 'pre-patriarchal' societies. Nevertheless, speculations about the nature of early societies and the reasons why males have been dominant in historical times continue to fascinate both utopian thinkers and apologists for male-dominated societies. Some researchers and theorists reconstruct pre-patriarchal cultures in order to model a non-patriarchal society and prove women capable of active and constructive participation in public life. Others are interested primarily in the conditions that led to the exclusion and suppression of women, often in the hope that such understanding will make it easier to achieve change in their own societies. In other words, because historians of matriarchy and patriarchy tend to have an agenda, their work needs to be seen as a form of utopian thinking as well as historical research.

The nature of matriarchy

Although non-Germans have contributed notably to the study of matriarchy—Robert Briffault, Bronislaw Malinowski and Robert Graves among them—the subject of matriarchy and its supposed supersession by patriarchy seems to have aroused exceptional interest in German-speaking countries. This may be due to Germany's strong Romantic tradition, with its cultural pessimism, its focus on the past as the site of original perfection, and its utopian hopes for a future that will reinstate that past. German Romanticism was revitalised by the political ideologies of the twentieth century.

The earliest and most influential theorist of a pre-patriarchal society was Swiss: Johann Jakob Bachofen (1948). In his 1861 study of 'Mother Right' (*Mutterrecht*), he proffered evidence for an early age of female dominance in the Mediterranean region. Bachofen, whose main sources were early historians, myths and archeological findings, assumed that matrilineality and matrilocality were indicators of a society in which women dominated, and that the primacy of female goddesses meant that women were held in high esteem. His research suggested that this 'gynaecocracy' (as he termed it) was characterised by almost utopian stability and peacefulness. But neither his sympathy with matriarchal culture nor his romantic nostalgia prevented him from seeing the rise of patriarchy as a release from stagnation, a coming of age of society and the start of progress. (Marielouise Janssen-Jurreit [1982:51ff.] presumes a little crudely that what motivated Bachofen's research was a Freudian mother-complex). Although his findings were not always understood or accepted, partly because they were ambivalent, they strongly influenced early twentieth-century German feminists like Helen Diner (1932, alias Sir Galahad), and Mathilde Vaerting (1975). Diner popularised what she thought were Bachofen's empowering ideas on matriarchy in her book on *Mütter und Amazonen*. For Mathilde Vaerting, who in 1921 had to invent a non-existent brother as her co-author in order to gain recognition for her research, matriarchy was a social system in which the gender roles had simply been reversed.

The most dedicated of the recent feminist researchers of matriarchy is Heide Göttner-Abendroth (1988, 1991a; also 1980, 1991b), whose latest work is a multi-volume study of the matriarchal cultures of the world. Her principal concern is to show that a consistent religious or cultic pattern pervades the rituals and social structures of all matriarchal cultures, and proves that matriarchy was originally universal. Examined closely, myths and fairy-tales from all cultures reveal adulterated traces of this original and (by implication) true form of spiritual and social organisation. In a painstakingly researched study, however, Beate Wagner (1982) suggests that at least in early Greek society the differences between matriarchy and patriarchy were much less defined than Göttner-Abendroth implies. They related to work practices, and there is no evidence that invasions by patriarchal warrior tribes destroyed this culture, as Göttner-Abendroth claims. Others are less sceptical. The philosopher Annegret Stopczyk (1991) draws on early philosophical and literary sources to construct pre-patriarchal thought as body-oriented and non-abstract. Carola Meier-Seethaler's history of matriarchy (1988) is written from the perspective of a psychotherapist daily confronted with clients distressed, confused or incapacitated by modern western society. A similar quest for a less repressive and destructive social system has motivated both Cillie Rentmeister's and Gerda Weiler's work on matriarchy. While Rentmeister (1985) seeks a more ecologically sensitive society, Weiler (1984, 1989) looks for social structures that give peace a better chance (Weiler, 1989). Such persistence—in spite of the inaccessibility of the material and the unlikelihood of conclusive results—suggests a powerful psychological need in many women to lay claim to a matriarchal culture and tradition in which they might have felt at home and can still take pride.

The origins of patriarchy

Men seem to have felt a comparable need to explain, justify or condemn the rise of patriarchy in order to solve or dispense with the vexed question of male dominance. Few are as fair-minded as the enlightened lawyer and administrator Theodor Gottlieb von Hippel (1979), whose speculative explanation of 1791 was intended to counter arguments that women are inferior. A century later, Friedrich Engels (1972) was less honest about his agenda. He argued in 1884 that the switch from matrilineal to patrilineal social structures was prompted by the need among private-property owning men to ensure that their legacies went to their own offspring. But as private property is also the prime target in communist critiques of society, Engels's analysis accorded rather too neatly with his political agenda. For many decades, it split the German feminist movement into a bourgeois and a socialist stream. Socialist women were convinced that, once communism had been installed, their problems as women in patriarchal conditions would be solved automatically and they could therefore defer consideration of these problems. Engels's theory has been elaborated by Ernest Bornemann (1975), whose ideas have also influenced feminists. Günter Dux (1992) sees the subordination of women as resulting inevitably from historical processes which enabled men (on account of their superior physical strength) to become the brokers of power but modern technology, he argues, has rendered these conditions obsolete. Another male theorist, the psychiatrist

Horst Eberhard Richter (1979), attributes male domination to men's loss of religious faith in the wake of the Enlightenment, and their consequent push to control a secular world. While women have been victims of men's insecurities, their social exclusion, Richter assures us, has enabled them to preserve emotional qualities that predestine them to become the healers and regenerators of men. Such ancillary roles, of course, are not new to women.

Most of the male theorists mentioned here analyse history with both a preconceived explanation and a congenial course of action in mind. These include giving equal rights and opportunities to women (Hippel); the abolition of private property (Engels and Bornemann); making way for women, now that the time is ripe (Dux); and feminising society (Richter). The female theorists, by contrast, are more open-minded and fatalistic. Both Regina Becker-Schmidt and Christina von Braun delve into history to discover the origins of women's oppression, but neither is under any illusion that historical inequities can be simply reversed. Though each attempts what resembles a grand theory, there is no foreclosure because they offer us no easy solutions. In a careful re-examination of research presented by Claude Meillassoux and Jean Baudrillard, Regina Becker-Schmidt (1987) investigates the bride trade as the possible origin of women's subordination, focusing on 'exchange' as a social transaction. A true exchange entails equivalence (neither party may exchange at the expense of the other); reciprocity (the agreement must be mutual); and reversibility (the roles of giver and taker must be reversible: both, therefore, must be free agents). Exchanges normally have two functions, one real and the other symbolic. As symbolic acts, exchanges are designed to bridge gaps, such as the one between life and death, which is thematised in initiation ceremonies. In early rural communities, bride-buying fulfilled a practical need: it provided optimum conditions for the reproduction of workers by balancing out and mixing the populations of small and otherwise closed sedentary groups.

The symbolic meaning of the exchange of brides, however, is not so obvious. What Becker-Schmidt finds strange is that women—whose reproductive capabilities were the commodity being traded, and who were useful as both productive and reproductive agents—neither controlled this trade not gained kudos from it. The answer lies in the incest taboo: in exchanging their virgin women, men in effect traded their sexual abstinence with regard to the women of their own group, and thereby became the perpetrators of the deal. Why would they go to the length of surrendering their sexual claim to these women in order to be actively involved in the transaction? Because exchange was a crucial regulator of social processes, it was in the interests of men to be included in it. Consequently, women (who on the real level embodied the value on which the exchange was based) lost out, and became (on the symbolic level) a mere vehicle of exchange, equivalent to a coin. And because social status was generated at the symbolic level, it was ultimately the women who suffered social death. The conditions of equivalence, reciprocity and reversibility were met on the symbolic level between men as partners, who traded abstinence for abstinence as free agents in a mutually agreed and reversible transaction whose outcome was homosocial bonding between two groups of men. Contrary to appearances, it was not a case of exchanging reproduction for reproduction. The custom of trading brides reified women in ways that determined their social status: they became a commodity because of their superior rather than their inferior value. According to Hannelore Schlaffer (1994), women (most commonly in the role of the beloved) are still being traded among men, who seek status by gaining one another's approval. The bride-trade is alive and well.

Christina von Braun (1985) put forward her theory of the origins of patriarchy in her comprehensive study of hysteria. Von Braun believes that the change from an egalitarian to a male-dominated society was a side effect of the invention of writing, which produced radical changes of mentality and culture. Her view is that the pre-patriarchal period was egalitarian, and characterised by a realistic attitude towards such facts of life as birth, death, regeneration and the interdependence of human beings as procreators and nurturers. All this changed with the invention of writing, which, by enabling names and stories to outlast people and their deeds, made it possible to conceive of eternal life. The gradual move towards abstraction can be observed in the change from a mimetic (pictographic) to an acoustic alphabet that relies on symbol. The great religions of the book (Judaism, Christianity and Islam) arose. They were based on faith in an invisible, spiritual and masculine god, on miracle, and on resurrection to eternal life. 'Truth' was no longer tangible and visible, but invisible, intangible and unreal. Because thinking began to be guided by hopes and wishes rather than observable realities, it became utopian. The new culture spawned new desires; prominent among them were autonomy, the overcoming of mortality, and the conquest of nature.

But what place did women have in this development, locked as they were into that regenerative cycle of birth and death, symbolically represented in older fertility cults? Men had symbolised human mortality in the old order, but it now became their role to identify not only with the transcendent and immortal spirit that had conquered death, but also with its medium, the written word. As custodians of the written word, men became the bearers of a culture of progress aimed at overcoming the limitations of nature. While women were associated with sexuality, materiality and death, men saw themselves as representing spirit, soul, transcendence, individuality, invention and eternal life. Paradoxically, patriarchal culture is intent on dissociating itself from physical fatherhood, as Bachofen had also observed. The cultural changes that accompanied the invention of writing thus led to an increasing loss of that sense of the real which relies on an acknowledgement of physicality. As the initial invention and adoption of the written word was achieved jointly by men and women, the male take-over was an unintended consequence of cultural change. In a later essay, von Braun (1989:69) hesitantly suggests that the situation could be reversed if women did not succumb to patriarchal images but reappropriated and embodied them. This would render such representations ambivalent, disconcerting and useless as prescriptions.

Alternative approaches to the origins of patriarchy investigate the psychological roots of sexism. Neither of the two theories summarised below could have been formulated without Freud's observations on the infant's relationship to the pre-Oedipal mother, as elaborated in Melanie Klein's object-relations psychology and the work of other women psychologists, such as Helene Deutsch, Anna Freud, Margaret Mahler, Janine Chasseguet-Smirgel, Dorothy Dinnerstein, Nancy Chodorow (1978) and Christiane Olivier. Collectively, as Christa Rhode-Dachser (1991b) has shown, they give increasing prominence to the aggressive power associated with the mother image (as distinct from the mother's actual role in life).

Interestingly, Judith Offenbach (1983) and Karin Walser (1984) evaluate the mother image very differently. Judith Offenbach, a lesbian academic who publishes under a pseudonym, begins with a puzzled examination of the social prohibition of homosexuality. Finding that neither western hostility to sexuality nor demographic imperatives provide a likely explanation, she finally turns for an answer to object-relations psychology, whose point of departure is deceptively simple. Every child's primary object of love is its mother, who remains the symbol of care and comfort. This means that the first love of both men and women is directed towards a woman; in other words, not only men but also women love women. Rejection, which appears to be man's natural destiny in love, can elicit a variety of responses. A rejected man can become dejected, and plead with the woman to accept him (romantic love); or he can turn away from women to a partner of his own sex; or react with hatred; or try to eliminate his desire for love and become autonomous; or try to compensate by bolstering his ego in other ways; or attempt to enforce love. All these forms of behaviour, Offenbach suggests, are widespread in men of almost all societies, and constitute the attitudes that lead to the formation of patriarchies. The prohibition of overt male homosexuality, Offenbach believes, is related to the fact that, because patriarchy is intrinsically although covertly homoerotic, societal and individual homoeroticism are in conflict with one another. Offenbach comes to the same conclusions as Nancy Chodorow, namely that joint parenting from the first moments of a child's life onwards is the most effective way of preventing those sexist attitudes which have such disastrous consequences for society.

For Karin Walser (1984) the pre-Oedipal mother is by no means a benign figure. Drawing on Renate Schlesier's (1990) contention that Greek myths grew out of the conflict between patriarchy and an earlier matriarchy, Walser assumes matriarchy to have been a period of sacrificial excess in which incest was not yet prohibited. Oedipus's ambivalence about the rising patriarchy is his downfall. Having destroyed the Sphinx (a matriarchal deity) with his masculinist answer to her riddle, he then kills Laios (a man whose homosexuality removed him from the influence of women) before reverting to the matriarchal custom of incest, with a suggestion that he is knowingly seduced by his mother. Symbolic castration (in the form of blinding) is effected by means of her brooch and not (as Freud had stipulated) through any threat emanating from his father. In much the same way as Oedipus, a young boy feels powerfully attracted to his mother, while at the same time fearing more than anything else her symbiotic power over him. In a bid to assert his autonomy, he escapes from the mother by rejecting and devaluing everything he associates with women, and by adopting an exaggerated form of masculinity. But flight is never a solution. Subconsciously, he continues to idealise his mother, and develops the counterpart of penis envy, namely a powerful desire to share in his mother's sexuality. Here Walser refers to a study by Bruno Bettelheim (1955) that relates both tribal initiation rites and the practices of severely disturbed young men to envy of the mother's reproductive powers. That envy is deeply suppressed in modern western society, though Walser thinks it resurfaces in the phenomenon of the 'Mappi', the father who pretends to be a mother.

For the girl too, the mother is the object of her first love. She must likewise escape from her mother to become an autonomous human being. To escape from your own sex, however, is even more difficult. The sisters of Orestes—Chrysothemis, Electra and Iphigenia—give us some insight into the problems girls face. Whereas Chrysothemis submits to her mother totally, Electra and Iphigenia rely on their brother to help them overcome their mother, Clytemnestra. None of the sisters undertakes the struggle on her own. In the end, Chrysothemis relinquishes all hope of autonomy, while Electra is consumed by hatred of her mother; only Iphigenia (who is also priestess to the goddess of birth, Artemis) succeeds in achieving some kind of balance. Just as boys devalue femininity in order to escape their mothers, so too girls may attempt to solve their problems by devaluing their own femininity and envying those boys whose struggle seems to be so much easier; in other words, by resorting to penis envy they can avoid coming to terms with their mothers. Yet the man seen as the knight in shining armour who will help the girl detach herself from the mother is also a threat, for he is the potential destroyer of the mother and thereby of all women. A woman both idealises a man and sees herself as his possible victim; this mirrors the relationship that a man has to his mother. But unlike men, women cannot resort to idealising their own sex. In this way, both sexes contribute to the patriarchal mentality of society, which is characterised on the one hand by an avoidance and rejection of the mother and all that is feminine, and on the other by an idealisation of masculinity that, in women, is coupled with fear and a sense of victimisation. The only solution, Walser argues, is an honest confrontation with the mother figure. But the mystification of motherhood that blocks out the mother's more sinister aspects (and which is characteristic of some sections of the women's movement) is unlikely to solve any problems. It is interesting to observe how feminist interpretations of the same phenomenon can be so diametrically opposed. Since presumably every child experiences the primal mother in both her positive and negative aspects, it is tempting to give both accounts their due. Patriarchy is a complex phenomenon, and the more insights and opinions at our disposal, the less likely we will be to come to premature and misleading conclusions.

The manifold varieties of sexism are documented historically by Marielouise Janssen-Jurreit in an encyclopaedic cross-cultural survey which was hailed as the first significant German contribution to international feminism when it was published in 1976. An abridged version was translated into English in 1982. Unlike the writers discussed so far, Janssen-Jurreit refuses to theorise about the origins of sexism, because to do so is to obscure the universality of the phenomenon and put women on the wrong track. Like other abuses of power, sexism is a disposition inherent in human society. The utopian belief in an egalitarian society of the future is misguided. More urgently needed are an awareness of patriarchal structures and a feminist political counter-force that tackles each problem in turn and resists being integrated into the patriarchal system. The structures and mechanisms of patriarchal domination as symptoms of a more basic disorder are examined in the next section. Relieving the symptoms is often a simpler task than remedying the underlying evil.

Mechanisms of control

The structures and mechanisms by means of which patriarchy exerts control over women are manifold. Gudrun-Axeli Knapp (1992) identifies five main dimensions of patriarchal power: the system of dominance, the symbolic order, institutions, interactions between individual men and women, and the socio-psychological effects of gender relationships. All are displayed as mechanisms of control in patriarchal structures.

Legal discrimination

As early as 1791 von Hippel (1979) drew attention to the absurdities and inequities of the law as it affected women. He laid the blame on Germany's borrowings from Roman family law, which placed all members under the *manus* ('hand': the German term was *Munt*) of the male head of the household. While young males could emancipate themselves by leaving the parental household, female home-leavers passed into the 'hand' of their husband or another male relative, without ever coming of age. Ute Gerhard (1986) has analysed historically the arguments used at various times to justify the *Munt*. Originally, women were seen to need protection because of their inability to defend themselves. Their inexperience and complaisance continued to be cited until the end of the nineteenth century when current legal philosophy made it possible to declare explicitly the interests of the man as head of the family. From the late eighteenth century onwards, however, the call for equality that came from revolutionary France acted as a counterbalance to the *Munt*. Thus the Prussian Code of 1794 was surprisingly liberal in its intentions (Gerhard, 1978). Yet in our century, although equal rights for men and women were written into the 1949 German constitution by the efforts of a female lawyer, Elisabeth Selbert, traditional family law remained operative for some years on, and tended to restrict women's rights on the basis of the customary divisions of labour. A ruling of 1953, for example, declared that although men and women had equal rights, their different tasks in relation to the family justified different treatment before the law; and in a contested inheritance in 1959, the male litigant was awarded the farm because he worked in the fields, whereas the woman (whose labours were indispensable to the running of the farm) worked largely in the house. Four years later, the Constitutional Court outlawed the privileging of males on the basis of traditional discriminatory work practices. Yet women still need to be vigilant, for as Barbara Böttger (1987) points out,. it will be some time before constitutional equality is adequately translated into law. Even equality before the law, however, is in itself not enough, for legal equality was rendered largely ineffectual in the GDR by widespread male chauvinism.

According to the German state and its institutional predecessors, the prime civil duty of women has always been to reproduce the population in a manner that assures effective care of the young. The three crucial mechanisms for perpetrating this belief were anchored in law as compulsory heterosexuality, legitimacy of offspring, and the prohibition of abortion (and at times even contraception). While legitimacy has dwindled in importance now that women have joined the work-force and can support their own children, the struggle for abortion rights has continued for most of the twentieth century. Though GDR women were granted what amounted to abortion on demand in 1973, those rights were lost again after the reunification of Germany. In 1993 the Constitutional Court ruled for the second time against a parliamentary decision to liberalise abortion by referring to its mandate to protect life. It is plain to women that the issues at stake are practical rather than ethical. Family duties tend to keep women out of a saturated employment market. Demographers worry about the negative birth rate among Germans (as against guest workers) and the concomitant problem of providing retirement security for growing numbers of elderly people. Although it has been difficult to come up with a principled defence of abortion rights, three different approaches have been suggested. The first stresses a woman's right to autonomy over her body as part of her right either to self-determination (which was the point made by the women campaigning against the constitutional prohibition in par.218 and by the European Parliament in 1990) or to freedom from harm, which is the position taken by Sichtermann (1986). The second stresses the right of a child to be wanted by its parents, and the potential social problem posed by unwanted children (Amendt, 1992); and the third attempts to determine the time at which a foetus becomes either a human being or an independent subject in law, whose rights are covered by the constitution. Barbara Duden's historical studies (1991b) show that for centuries the first movement of the foetus was deemed to be the moment when it gained human status; consequently, a woman was not considered with child in the first months of her pregnancy when decisions about abortion had to be made. By contrast, medical technology today can register a pregnancy at the moment of conception. Women are expected nowadays to submit to monitoring and to adjust their life-style (most recently under threat of legal sanctions) without having any period of private decision-making, as Wolfgang van den Daele (1988) points out. Two judges on the 1975 bench of the Constitutional Court registered their dissenting opinion that, because the protection of life is achieved far more effectively by providing social support, the constitution does not require prohibitions to be put in place (Schwarzer, 1986). The prominence of the pro-abortion campaign in the German women's movement suggests that German feminists perceive lack of control over their bodies as one of the most serious hurdles they have to overcome.

Although homosexuality is no longer outlawed, the law has been slow to consider marital, adoption and property rights for homosexual couples. Alice Schwarzer (1977) has speculated about reasons why heterosexuality remains dominant. She argues that because vaginal penetration is regarded as the only truly hetero-sexual practice, what Anne Koedt (1973) calls the 'myth of the vaginal orgasm' becomes the essential mechanism for maintaining patriarchal dominance. Although sexual pleasure can obviously be achieved in homosexual relationships, women are led to believe that they are sexually in need of men, so that the heterosexual hegemony (and all the domestic and child-rearing services that go with it under patriarchy) will not be called into question. This shows that laws need to be demythologised before they can be changed.

Economic discrimination

Like Freud, Marx has been perceived by feminists as both an enlightener (in critiquing economic exploitation and class structures) and a deceiver (in remaining oblivious to the economic value of women's work). One of the first feminists to criticise Marx's definition of work was Hannelore Mabry (1977). She points out that Marx falsely links productivity (in the sense of surplus value) to wage labour, whereas in fact such practices as slave labour, corvée (unpaid labour), housework and child rearing are also productive, since the owner of this labour profits from it either directly through overtime or from indirect economies in his labour power. Marx erred in rejecting 'labour saving' as an economic factor, and in assuming that the reproduction and regeneration of the work-force do not contribute to the economy. Furthermore, Marx refused to see that housework is equivalent structurally to slave labour. His belief that men not alienated by capitalism would be innately fair ignored the fact (to which Engels drew attention) that the first division of labour—and with it the earliest practices of exploitation—was effected by men against women. It was through such exploitation (and the surplus value it produced) that private property first came into existence. By using gender-neutral concepts, Marx disguised the fact that he ought to have targeted not the family but women, not capital or hierarchy but patriarchy, and not one class system but two, differentiated by gender. Mabry calculates that a working mother with three children creates surplus value for ten hours of each working day, that a 'kept' wife works two hours less than her subsistence cost, and that the average man does subsistence work for five hours a day and creates surplus value for three. Accounting systems based solely on wage labour render invisible the economic contribution to society by women, and deny them their due recognition. Mabry points out the value of Dalla Costa's call for 'wages for housewives' (1975), if only as an interim measure.

The exclusion of traditional women's work from economic theory both reflects and creates a false consciousness that affects perceptions of women, their actual place in society and their opportunities for bettering themselves. Gudrun-Axeli Knapp argues that if women's labour and its contribution to society are to be assessed properly, the Marxian categories of 'labour power' and the 'commodity of labour power' need to be supplemented by two less narrowly economic categories, namely 'subject potentials' and 'subjective labour potential'. 'Subject potentials' she defines as 'the totality of aptitudes, abilities, capabilities and needs that have developed biographically in the course of processes of socialisation and individuation differentiated according to gender and class' (Knapp, 1987:273, my trans.). 'Subjective labour potential' comprises everything that the subject could contribute to the practice of society: hence production here includes all aspects of life. By means of her supplementary categories, Knapp believes, it is possible to assess more fairly the potential and actual economic and non-economic contributions made by individuals to society, as well as to show how present-day society wastes individual potential.

A group of three German sociologists—Maria Mies, Claudia von Werlhof and Veronika Bennholdt-Thomsen—who have worked together for many years and whose studies are largely available in English translation, have a similar critique of Marx's economic theory which they have substantiated by years of research in various Third World countries (Mies et al., 1988). They too make the point that the surplus value of capitalism derives mainly from the unpaid (and consequently invisible) labour not only of women but also of people in colonised Third World countries who work in the informal or subsistence sectors. Marxist theory overlooks these workers by defining them and their work as natural resources, which are not acquired but appropriated. But capitalism would never have developed without them. Its rise coincides not only with the colonisation and appropriation of territories but also with the exclusion of women from paid work at the beginning of the bourgeois period of industrialisation.

Capitalism is bound up inextricably with the 'housewifisation' (*Hausfrauisierung*) of women and the equivalent exploitation of colonial peoples.

The mechanism of housewifisation works as follows. The poorer the country or the more severe the economic crisis—which more often than not is created by the colonial powers through loans, conditions attached to them, and interest to be paid—the larger the informal and non-wage-earning sector becomes. These people then provide the labour pool on which capitalism can draw. Because the housewife and the subsistence farmer are by definition unpaid, their occasional wage labour can be remunerated at very low rates. Thus young women working in multi-national factories can be paid a pittance because they are only filling in time before becoming housewives, whose work is totally unremunerated. Because housewives are unpaid, what they do tends not to be classified as real work; consequently, they are expected to take on additional money-earning work, like the lace-makers of Narsapur (Mies, 1982). Confined to their homes, these women are paid next to nothing for long hours of additional work. Their husbands, who trade their wives' produce while themselves not being productive, thus adopt the role of capitalist entrepreneur, and often better their wage and social status at the expense of their wives.

Though housewifisation and such equivalents as subsistence farming or informal work are very much more widespread in colonised countries, they are also an essential part of the western socio-economic system. The economic superiority of western countries is based on the fact that they can exploit both their colonies and their women. 'It is my thesis', Mies concludes, 'that capitalism cannot function without patriarchy, that the goal of this system, namely the never-ending process of capital accumulation, cannot be achieved unless patriarchal man–woman relations are maintained or newly created' (Mies et al., 1988:2). Marxism is exposed as pursuing the interests of the male wage-labourer, and consequently implicated not only in the suppression of women but also in the exploitation of colonies.

While housewifisation developed as a mechanism for controlling and exploiting women in conditions of early capitalism, contemporary German women (in both the East and the West) have their own problems. Prior to reunification, Irene Dölling (1989) was one of the few East German academic sociologists with a feminist perspective. While conceding that the GDR put in place many of the necessary measures to ensure social equality for women, she points out that it did nothing about their double work-load. Most women were in employment; they had access to education and child care, they could take time off when they needed to care for children, and they had abortion rights. Nevertheless, women remained disadvantaged because equal rights and economic independence had not altered traditional expectations of them inculcated at an early age. As a result, women were overworked, constantly had to compromise in matters related to their jobs and training, and were deprived not only of the leisure due to them but also of the time to become involved in politics. In addition, they were also often dissatisfied with the care they could give their families. In interpreting these findings, Dölling refers to the contradictions expected in a transitional period of socialism.

Equal employment opportunities, like equal aspirations towards independence and self-fulfilment tend to result in the double work-load, and are problematic in other respects too. This point— merely touched upon by Dölling—has been discussed more expansively by the West German couple Elisabeth Beck-Gernsheim and Ulrich Beck (1989). In their sociological study they examined what happens to the stability of personal relationships and family life when both partners subscribe to an individualistic code of values, in defiance of earlier and more rigid marital prescriptions that ruled out paid work for women. Interviews with female factory workers conducted by Regina Becker-Schmidt and others (1984) draw attention to the psychological difficulties entailed in switching back and forth between the entirely different expecta-tions and demands of workplace and family. Without far more radical changes to the gender-based division of work, women are likely to remain disadvantaged one way or the other.

Practices of exclusion

Traditionally, women have been excluded from what Jürgen Habermas (1989) calls the 'public sphere', that is from political, judicial, cultural and economic life. Von Hippel (1979) had argued in 1791 that since men's interests were at stake, it was absurd to explain or excuse this practice in terms of women's 'natural modesty'. Carola Lipp (1986) has shown how, in the mid nineteenth century, working-class women who had taken to doing their work on the streets for company (and were impertinent enough to comment openly on what was going on around them) were forced back into their houses. But twentieth-century male theorists of the public sphere have tended to overlook the gender factor (Schlüpmann, 1990). Marxist critics usually assume that women's problems would be solved by the abolition of the private sphere. Ulrike Prokop (1978) points out, however, that if productivity is taken to include what is socially necessary and desirable (as was actually the case in Marx's early work) then housework—with its emphasis on the satisfaction of needs, its co-operative rather than competitive practices, and its concern with human relations—constitutes an indispensable kind of productivity. Like industrial efficiency, which has a utopian potential to make wealth more widely available, the care and co-operation that characterise domestic work show us the way to a better society. Both forms of labour, of course, also produce psychological problems; women, for instance, are socialised to be self-sacrificial (Prokop, 1978; Vedder-Shults, 1978). Alluding to Habermas in the title of her examination of 'structural changes in the private sphere' Kornelia Hauser (1987) likewise exposes the inadequacies of traditional social theory in focusing exclusively on the public sphere. But in so far as the private sphere is a sanctuary for both men and women from the dehumanising public sphere, it further entrenches capitalism. If the contradictions of society are to be confronted and resolved, Hauser argues, the boundaries between public and private must become fluid, and all members of society should participate actively and responsibly in both. To involve more women in the paid work-force and more men in parenting are steps in the right direction. A collection of essays (1992) published by women who call themselves the *Gruppe feministische Öffentlichkeit* (group for a feminist public sphere) takes a critical look at the impact feminist ideas and practices have had on the media, and specifically on the extent to which the media emulate (in their focus on people) the traditional feminine medium of gossip. They find that feminist media work is often characterised by those fluid boundaries between public and private which Hauser advocates.

An effective mechanism for locking women out of the public sphere in present-day Germany is the half-day school system, with its emphasis on supervised homework. In the absence of those after-school programmes available in the former GDR, working mothers are often unable to provide their schoolchildren with adequate supervision, and therefore tend to be blamed for youth violence and other social problems. Surprisingly, an extension and reorganisation of the school day has not been prominent on feminist agendas.

Other exclusionary practices, such as those deriving from Freudian psychoanalysis, are more subtle. As a doctor, Freud was aware that the society he practised in was asking women to make themselves ill by cultivating a passivity that would suit their male partners. Nevertheless, as a therapist he induced women to conform to his own and society's expectations of them. Perceiving women to be inferior in their lack of male characteristics, Freud refused to acknowledge they had separate sexual needs. Freud's ideas were in many respects useful and inspiring. But because they were so widely disseminated, the prejudices they spread were particularly insidious. The feminist critique of Freud was initiated by Karen Horney (1967) in essays on the psychology of women published between 1922 and 1936 (see also Stephan, 1992). In Germany, it has been elaborated by Renate Schlesier (1990) and Christa Rhode-Dachser (1991a).

The feminist linguist Luise Pusch (1984) has analysed German as a *Männersprache* moulded by and suited to the needs of men, a language in which women are forced to identify with the male perspective because the generic is invariably masculine. Similarly, the writer Verena Stefan (1979) points out that the vocabulary of sexuality is largely unacceptable to women because it is shaped by male perspectives which hinder them from talking about their own sexual feelings and needs. The more aggressive speech habits of men also contribute to the silencing of women, as Senta Trömel-Plötz (1982) shows.

In addition to language, the prescriptive theorisation of gender has done much to exclude women from culture and power. Even the 'feminine' virtues were not securely in the possession of women. Although initially the less socially desirable qualities were usually ascribed to women, evaluations could change with historical circumstances. Men who expressed admiration for 'feminine' virtues did not necessarily esteem women, and often were less interested in sharing these virtues than in appropriating them. The nineteenth-century philosopher Schopenhauer (1974), for instance, who teaches that the will (that driving force of the active masculine life) should be negated through recourse to beauty, compassion and mysticism (all traditionally feminine qualities) published in 1851 one of the most misogynous tracts of his gynophobic century. Because Schopenhauer takes possession of all positive human qualities in the name of man, he inevitably reduces Woman to a despicable nothing, a mere reproductive machine. We should never forget that the admiration or rehabilitation of 'femininity' has often resulted in the exclusion or destruction of women.

This explains why the writings of Herbert Marcuse, who presents himself as a convert to feminism (1974), have had a guarded response from feminists like Mabry (1977). For Marcuse, the 'feminine' qualities of receptivity, sensitivity, non-violence and tenderness, which he ascribes to women, are a redemptive force in society. Men should acquire them in order to become better and fairer rulers of society. Feminism is a revolt against moribund capitalism. Ideologically pre-defined real women should be co-opted into the service of the patriarchal project of socialism, which is in need of regeneration and amendment. It is women's mission to humanise men. What Marcuse calls 'feminist socialism' is in reality 'feminine socialism'.

Theories of the good woman tend to imagine women as motherly healers and carers who selflessly forgive the waywardness of men. Such strategies can be effective, as is evident from a recent anthology in which women from ethnic minority groups in Germany were asked to write on war as a male obsession (Schwarzer, 1992). All attribute the sufferings of their kinswomen to the understandable frustrations of men, whose egos have been injured by class divisions, colonial domination, or the selfish interests of western industrialism. Maja Nadig (1986), an ethno-psychoanalyst, reports that Mexican women tolerate machismo because it enables formerly independent men to vent their frustrations with western economic intervention without losing face. While that may be valid as a short-term solution for hard-pressed women who want to appease their men, it nevertheless reinforces the assumption that men are the naturally dominant sex. What complicates the problem of patriarchy is the fact that women have strong and multiple commitments to men, whose interests often cannot be separated from their own.

Femininity and Beyond: Reframing Female Subjectivity

What is *Weiblichkeit?*

Despite the fact that German, like French, has only one word for 'female' and 'feminine' (*weiblich*) and one for 'sex' and 'gender' (*Geschlecht*), it has been conventional in German feminist theory to distinguish the *Weiblichkeit* given by 'nature' from that which is socially constructed. However, the extent and significance of biological differences between the sexes— and the precise meanings, values and modes of (re-)production of 'femininity' as a cultural norm to which women are expected to conform—have been hotly debated. Moreover, how such questions have been approached in theory is closely connected with the varying strategic choices and utopian goals that have emerged within German feminism as a political movement.

As detailed in Chapter 1, German feminists have analysed femininity in relation to the dialectic of enlightenment, partly as a function of the emergence of the bourgeois nuclear family and the dissociation of public from private spheres, and partly as the fantasised Other of the discourse of masculine reason. Such studies represent only a small fraction of the German feminist research into the construction of Woman in western (and particularly German) culture following the publication in 1977 of Silvia Bovenschen's influential work on 'imagined femininity', a concept which has played an important role in both German feminist historiography (described in Chapter 2) and research on those artistic and literary 'images of woman' to be discussed in Chapter 5.

Here, however, I would like to focus on the counterpart of this critique of 'man-made' woman: namely, feminist theorisations of female subjectivity. I have separated these into three key areas: sexuality and motherhood, productivity, and thought and language. In the final section of this chapter I delineate the main lines of dispute in discussions of femininity by considering the German reception of two influential and mutually contradictory models of gender and subjectivity: the reaffirmation of female difference in the Italian *affidamento* movement, and the dissolution of the sex–gender distinction in recent North American feminist theory.

Sexuality and motherhood

Because sexuality and motherhood are central to the social and cultural construction of femininity, it is hardly surprising that they also play an important role in feminist endeavours to rethink female subjectivity.

In the FRG, the campaign to liberalise the abortion law and increase access to contraception placed motherhood firmly (albeit negatively) on the feminist agenda. The slogan 'My belly belongs to me!' indicated not only that women wanted the right to chose when and whether to have a child, but also that motherhood should not be regarded as every woman's desire and destiny. Coupled with this distancing from (and in some cases violent rejection of) the role of mother was a desire to liberate female sexuality from the risk of unwanted pregnancy as well as from those strictures and deformations to which patriarchy subjects it. By the early 1980s, however, a reorientation was evident in German feminist criticism. 'Sexuality' (and especially 'sexual liberation') was seen as more problematic than had initially been assumed, and 'motherhood' revalued as a positive manifestation of female subjectivity.

Celebrating the clitoris—mourning the vagina

Although a German translation of Simone de Beauvoir's *Le deuxième sexe* appeared in 1968—to be followed by Kate Millet's *Sexual Politics* in 1970, Germaine Greer's *The Female Eunuch* in 1971, and Anne Koedt's 'Myth of Vaginal Orgasm' in 1974— German discussions of the sexual repression of women did not get under way until the publication in 1975 of a book called *Der kleine Unterschied und seine großen Folgen* (The Small Difference and Its Big Consequences) by Alice Schwarzer (1977). This is a collection of interviews with sixteen women of different ages, social backgrounds and marital status, concerning their relationships (especially sexual) with men, followed by some polemical essays on the 'function of sexuality in the repression of women' and the 'double burden' of working women. It quickly became a best seller. As Schwarzer emphasises in her commentaries, the burden of these 'protocols' is clear. Sexual relations between men and women do not offer the fulfilment promised by the discourses either of romantic love or (more recently) the kind of 'sexual liberation' promoted within the student movement of the 1960s. For the women interviewed, sex was a form of imprisonment. Moreover, the impression given is that this was not only due to structural inequalities between the sexes, but also to the fact that male and female sexual needs were intrinsically incompatible. A not uncommon response to this perception within the West German women's movement was to turn away from men altogether. For if (as Koedt and Schwarzer argue) female orgasm is produced by the clitoris and not the vagina, men and their overrated appendages were superfluous to women's sexual pleasure.

The critique of compulsory heterosexuality has contributed decisively to the development of a lively and increasingly pluralistic lesbian counterculture, especially in the larger cities of the German-speaking area—although lesbianism was already seen (and to some extent still is) as a political choice rather than merely a sexual preference. However, while the 'discovery' of the clitoris promised sexual autonomy to women, it is perhaps unfortunate that this was coupled with a negation of the vagina. This point was made by Renate Schlesier (1984), who argued that feminist critics of the allegedly Freudian 'myth of vaginal orgasm' were actually closer to their *bête noire* Freud than they realised. For Freud (1977, 1983) too recognises clitoral orgasm only—albeit as an 'infantile' and 'masculine' stage of female sexual development— while referring to the vagina as the site of that 'lack' or 'castration wound', which makes it a passive receptacle for the satisfaction of male desire. Schlesier had previously published a highly regarded (and recently republished) critical analysis of Freud's psychoanalytical demythologisation and remythologisation of femininity, especially in relation to his studies on hysteria (Schlesier, 1990). In this article, however, her primary target is Freud's feminist critics, who had unwittingly reiterated his negation (*Totsagung*, literally 'pronouncing dead') of the vagina by defining coitus exclusively in terms of male penetration, and failing to recognise the interconnectedness of clitoral and vaginal arousal in female orgasm. If this kind of self-negation is the price of emancipation then (as Schlesier puts it in the title of her article) it is indeed a cause for mourning (*Trauerarbeit*).

'Generative sexuality' and the 'new motherliness'

Feminist theory and lesbianism, which came together briefly in the critique of compulsory heterosexuality, went their separate ways in the FRG in the late 1970s. Only recently has a new *rapprochement* begun. For this and other reasons—such as the ageing of the first generation of the second women's movement, and, arguably, the cultural and political conservatism of the Kohl era (Helmut Kohl's Christian Democratic Party came to power in 1983)—German feminist discussions of sexuality during the 1980s were dominated by two new projects: the theorisation of a non-exploitative heterosexuality, and the reaffirmation of motherhood as a positive dimension of female subjectivity and erotic experience.

Both are evident in the work of Barbara Sichtermann (1986), whose collection of essays, *Femininity* (first published in German in 1983), has also been translated into English. Like Schlesier, Sichtermann is critical of 1970s celebrations of the clitoris. In her view, these negated not only the vagina, but also the role of fantasy and 'narrative'—provided by the history of a relationship, however brief or long—in sexual pleasure, and reduced eroticism to mere mechanics. According to Sichtermann, the kind of sexual unhappiness documented by Schwarzer originates in the misfit between women's new sense of self and those old roles that were still being played out in sexual encounters between men and women. Since giving up altogether on the opposite sex is not a satisfactory solution for most women, Sichtermann proposes the dissolution of these fixed positions into a range of non-gendered 'behavioural possibilities' and 'variations'. These would enable women to assume an active role in constituting men as objects of desire, while allowing men to enjoy the narcissistic pleasures of passivity for a change. In developing a new culture of female desire, Sichtermann none the less also argues that biology should be given its due, if not as 'fate', then at least as 'condition of possibility' and 'limit'. The importance of appreciating the dialectical interplay of biology and society, nature and history, especially at a time when the consequences of overstepping ecological limits could be disastrous, is dealt with in the first essay of her 1987 collection *Wer ist wie?* In earlier essays (1986) she had already argued that our understanding of female sexuality should be extended to include the irrational desires and erotic possibilities connected with conception, pregnancy, childbirth and breast-feeding—and especially (as she is careful to emphasise in her essays on the 'desire for children' and the 'lost eroticism of the breast') where child-bearing is a matter of choice.

Sichtermann's transgression of the feminist taboo on biological arguments, especially with regard to the desire for children, was highly controversial in the FRG, where it was seen as playing into the hands of conservatives who wanted women sent back to their 'rightful place' in the home. However, by comparison with texts such as Gisela Erler's *Frauenzimmer: Für eine Politik des Unterschieds* (1985), which is more typical of the affirmation not only of women's procreative bodies but also, and above all, of their identity and role as mother, Sichtermann's notion of 'generative sexuality' attempts a careful balancing act. It is coupled with a strong reaffirmation of the importance of the right to abortion on demand as an extension of the right to freedom from bodily harm, and in recognition of the fact that the ability to decide when and if to have a child is a precondition for women's emancipation. Moreover, the fact that women have a monopoly on procreation does not mean that they should be exclusively responsible for child care. In fact, in her earlier books on this subject, Sichtermann (1981, 1982) argues that it is best for all concerned if this task is shared between two and preferably more adults. Her reconceptualisation of mothering as potentially erotic departs significantly from conventional constructions of motherhood according to what Hilge Landweer (1990) terms the martyr model. The dichotomisation of female identity into either a selfless and asexual mother or the erotic object of desire is a characteristically patriarchal strategy that was particularly prevalent in the nineteenth century. In that context, Sichtermann's call for an eroticisation of reproduction was truly subversive.

Feminist reappropriations and redefinitions of pregnancy, childbirth and mothering as a potentially positive dimension of female subjectivity are perhaps all the more important in view of the ever-increasing medicalisation and technologisation of procreation. However, in some feminist critiques of IVF and gene technology, which are particularly strident in the FRG, the desire to preserve the female monopoly on reproduction could be seen to resurrect what earlier feminists had regarded as a problematic identification of women with motherhood and nature. As Mona Singer (1988:123, my trans.) observes, the 'strategy of "save what you can" might work as a kind of first-aid (re)action, but offers no perspective for radical change'. And yet, quite apart from their wider social and ethical implications, these biomedical developments certainly threaten women's generative sexuality (Konnertz, 1988:13). Barbara Duden (1991b) has also pointed out that the discourses surrounding IVF programmes—and the increasingly routine medical surveillance of foetal development—have something in common with the rhetoric of anti-abortionists: namely, a tendency to represent the pregnant woman's body as a special environment, in which society has a legitimate interest, and which must therefore be carefully maintained—and utilised—in order to foster the life within it. As a historian of the body, Duden traces this problematic tendency back to around 1800, when women's wombs began to be constructed in medical and juridical discourses as a public space at precisely the same time that moral and civic discourses were identifying women themselves with the private sphere.

Female sexualisation

During the 1980s a very different theory of female sexuality from Sichtermann's was being developed by two socialist feminists, Frigga Haug and Kornelia Hauser. They argued in a series of books—two of which have appeared in English (Haug et al., 1987; Haug, 1992)—that sexuality itself is implicated systematically in female oppression. This is different from that direct subjection to male sexual appetite which Alice Schwarzer had theorised. Haug and Hauser see women as neither simply the victims of external power structures nor as essentially free agents. Instead they focus on the role played by sexuality in female identity-formation, or 'subjectification', defined as the 'process whereby individuals work themselves into social structures they themselves do not consciously determine, but to which they subordinate themselves' (Haug et al., 1987:59). For girls and women, this involves the progressive 'sexualisation' of all parts of the female body—and the development of an identity and corresponding behavioural traits (emotively labelled 'slave-girl')—which positions them as objects of male desire. Such an identity might well confer a degree of power and pleasure, at least for a while and in some situations; but the price is high, because it curtails women's intellectual and social development, and alienates them from their bodies. While subjectification 'allows for the active participation of individuals in heteronymy' (ibid.), the repressive sexualisation of the body can be countered through a process Haug and Hauser term 'memory work'. At once a research method and a form of group therapy, this will be discussed in detail in Chapter 8.

Following Foucault, Haug and Hauser see the problem of emancipatory change as involving liberation not *of* but *from* sexuality as constituted within those social discourses which 'discipline' the body. Hauser points out, however, that for women at least there can be no Foucauldian reclamation of 'bodies and pleasures', because the female body is itself the site and effect of women's sexual socialisation (ibid.:204–5). For this reason, Haug and Hauser are critical of the feminist 'culture of the body', which they believe risks reaffirming the identification of women with sexuality. Moreover, in keeping with their socialist affiliations, they also 'go beyond' Foucault by arguing that the discourse of sexuality is ideological, in that it legitimates and reinforces particular social relations which can and must be overthrown in the interests of creating a truly free society.

Productivity

The notion that there is a distinctive mode of female productivity arises from reflections on the social consequences of women's child-bearing capacity. Achieving prominence in the mid 1980s in the FRG, it signals a shift away from the feminist enlightenment view that the domestic sphere has only negative value as the site of women's imprisonment. From the perspective of a feminist critique of patriarchal civilisation in terms of the domination and exploitation of women and nature, women's domestic 'subsistence production'—as Mies, von Werlhof and Bennholdt-Thomsen (1988) have termed their controversial theory (discussed in Chapter 3)—might constitute an alternative, and superior model of productivity. This possibility is also explored in a 1980 essay by Brigitte Wartmann (1984) on the 'other' productivity of women. Her point of departure is a critique of the historical association of women with nature, and the corresponding designation of their work in the home as mere reproduction. Wartmann argues that women's domestic labour—including housekeeping, as well as pregnancy, childbirth and child-rearing—is a cultural praxis that destabilises such polarisations as production–reproduction and human endeavour–natural processes. By contrast with the dominant model of male productivity, the culture of women's work does not seek to transcend the body or dominate nature. It is a labour of or with the body (*leiblich-sinnliche Arbeit*), which daily produces anew the material basis for human life. Excluded from the project of cultural and social progress, which none the less remains dependent upon the unacknowledged domestic production of women, their work and subjectivity, Wartmann argues, is more embodied than men's. This point is made also by Julia Kristeva (1976b) in an interview often cited by German theorists of 'feminine' productivity, including Wartmann. Wartmann, however, is wary of other French variants of this notion, such as Hélène Cixous' celebration of the female body as the privileged locus of women's freedom. Because women's bodies and domestic labour have always been subjected to patriarchal domination and exploitation, Wartmann warns against celebrating feminine productivity and corporeality in themselves. Instead, we should endeavour to dissolve the public–private split, and thus transform feminine productivity from an unfree private into a liberated social praxis (Wartmann, 1984:28), in which, presumably, both men and women would be free to participate.

Thought and language

Historically, women's thought and language have been constituted as the negative counterpart of an allegedly universal discourse of reason. As illogical thinkers whose hearts dominated their heads, and whose speech was incoherent, women were long excluded not only from philosophical speculation but also from institution-alised intellectual endeavour in general. In Germany, women did not gain the right to enrol in and graduate from university until 1908. In order to be taken seriously, it has been important for women to deny that their powers of intellect and expression are either inferior to or in any way different from those of men. Assertions of intellectual equality underlie feminist critiques of the conclusions frequently drawn from research into brain functions, which proves that in women the right (holistic) hemisphere predominates, whereas the left (analytic) hemisphere is more important in men. Helga Andresen (1988:15, my trans.) denounces such findings as the 'pseudo-scientific legitimation of conventional prejudgements'.

As Carol Hagemann-White observes, the feminist enlightenment goal of participating as men's equals in the public exercise of reason has coexisted uneasily with feminist critiques of the dominant (androcentric) model of rational thought and language (1989:13). Such critiques are frequently tied to the notion that women are, or should become, the source of a different kind of rationality. Hagemann-White identifies three main ways of grounding feminine thought: in women's bodies, in their work, or in their early psychosocial development. Marianne Schuller (1990d) adds a fourth: the discursive and institutional positioning of women as Other. She argues for a model of women's intellectuality that neither conforms to prevailing norms of patriarchal knowledge nor instantiates an essentially female intellectual difference. If women experience discomfort with the institutionalised discourse of reason because they sense that their participation in it is conditional on the suppression of their sexual identity then, according to Schuller, that constitutes the grounds for a radical feminist critique of the existing nexus of power and knowledge. Following Julia Kristeva (1976a), Schuller locates the subversive potential of women's thought in its alterity, or otherness, which situates it outside those binary oppositions inscribed within patriarchal forms of knowledge and enables it to disclose the vested interests that this knowledge both serves and masks.

Although Schuller's model of female intellectuality as feminist critique avoids the pitfalls of biological determinism, it leaves two questions unanswered: from what position, and to what end, is the feminist critique of power and knowledge to be launched? By contrast with such a negative or ascetic approach, other German feminists have begun to ask what positive differences women might contribute to the feminist transformation of thought and language. This project underlies Brigitte Nölleke's claim (1985) that women's thought structures are not linear, but typically move in 'all directions at once'. Although Hagemann-White classifies Nölleke's wide-ranging study with body-based theories, Nölleke ultimately places greater emphasis on women's domestic work. Nölleke argues that because the modern home serves the interests of commodity production, as well as being targeted by advertising, the thinking of housewives is influenced by what Marxists term 'commodity fetishism': that is, the tendency to assess objects merely in terms of their market value. Yet to the extent that the domestic sphere remains in some ways continuous with pre-modern subsistence production, women's everyday thinking and language also retain elements of an archaic magical, mimetic mode of thought which could be drawn upon to counter the hegemony of instrumental reason.

A more truly body-based approach than Nölleke's is to be found in Annegret Stopczyk's *Leibphilosophie* (1991). Originally presented as a series of radio broadcasts, Stopczyk's philosophy of embodiment critiques the logocentric and life-denying tradition of western thought inaugurated by Socrates (and especially his pupil Plato) and proposes a new approach to knowledge, based on bodily experience in all its gendered particularity. Women can contribute uniquely to the philosophy of embodiment because their capacity to give birth gives them insights into the value of all life as something both individuated and interconnected. Such insights are either suppressed or distorted under patriarchy. Feminine knowledge, which Stopczyk refers to as Sophia (wisdom, as distinct from Logos, the law) is thus as yet a utopian possibility rather than a reality.

Fearing a renewed idealisation of motherhood as women's true calling, other German-speaking theorists of feminine rationality have linked their project less closely to childbirth than Stopczyk does. Several share her commitment, however, to a re-embodiment of reason. For example, the prominent Austrian philosopher Brigitte Weißhaupt (Weißhaupt, 1983, 1986a, 1986b, 1989, 1990) grounds her proposed feminisation of reason partly in the different psychosocial development and historical experience of women, and partly in their discursive association with the suppressed and repressed. She draws eclectically upon Critical Theory, French philosophy and social theory (Derrida, Kristeva, Irigaray, Foucault, Lyotard) and American feminist theories of women's psychological and moral standpoint (Nancy Chodorow and Carol Gilligan). Like Schuller, she seeks to go beyond that polarisation of positions which offers a false choice between an uncritical feminist appropriation of the discourse of reason and an undialectical celebration of its antithesis. She proposes that women should turn to advantage that history of cultural representation and social conditioning which earlier feminists rightly criticised as a source of female oppression. Since, traditionally, women have been positioned in greater proximity to the realm of embodied being, but are now beginning to find their voice(s), women are today well placed to bring about what Weißhaupt calls a 'Sensitiver-Werden der Vernunft' (a sensitisation or sensualisation of reason) (1990:152). Similarly, Christine Kulke, in her critical engagement with the *Dialectic of Enlightenment*, calls for the development of a form of a 'sinnliche Vernunft' (sensuous reason) to counter the patent irrationality of the dominant mode of instrumental reason (Kulke, 1988a, 1988b, 1989, 1990). Neither Weißhaupt nor Kulke advocates blind subjection to feeling and sensuality, but rather their cultural mediation. In this sense, sensuous reason constitutes a form of communicative action, albeit of a rather different kind from the decidedly disembodied model of communicative action theorised by Habermas (1984) as offering a way out of the dialectic of enlightenment. Like many Anglo-American feminists (for example, in Meehan, 1995), Kulke (1988b) is critical of Habermas' gender-blindness, and she argues that his theory depends upon presuppositions that reinscribe the polarisation of the sexes, while failing to account for the emergence of domination in communicatively structured situations (ibid.:66–8). Whereas communicative action, Habermas-style, aims at the articulation of new universal norms and values, sensuous reason involves giving voice to those particularities of embodied experience, in which all thought and language is embedded, that have been silenced in the long history of ratiocentric enlightenment. In Weißhaupt's terms, this process of mediation involves speaking from inside the shadow that falls back upon reason, a shadow created by that which reason's light has obscured. Speaking from this shadow, feminist philosophy contributes to that postmodern transition which Jean-François Lyotard calls the 'self-overcoming' of enlightenment (cited in Weißhaupt, 1990:154), namely the liberation from domination by only one of a potential plurality of rationalities. Feminist philosophy, as Weißhaupt understands it, promotes a political programme of emancipation that will steer a path for women between the Scylla of a feminine over-identification with nature and the body and the Charybdis of the patriarchal subjugation of both.

The body in question

Underlying the discussions of female subjectivity are fundamental disagreements as to whether gender difference is socially constructed or biologically grounded, and whether 'femininity' is something that feminists should seek to overcome or rather revalue, redefine or even rediscover. Related to all this is an even deeper ideological difference, which (characteristically of ideology) is frequently not spelt out: namely, between those who see humanity—in its limitless malleability and hence manipulability—as radically divorced from nature, and those who believe that humanity's survival depends upon a new awareness of our ecological and bodily limits.

The German reception of two new developments in feminist theory—one Italian, the other American—highlights these fundamental differences. The Italian or *affidamento* approach, based on the later work of Luce Irigaray, was developed by women connected with the women's bookshop in Milan and the feminist philosophers' group in Verona called 'Diotima'. In their two books on women's freedom and sexual difference, which appeared in German translation in 1989 (Milan Women's Bookstore Collective, 1990; Diotima, 1991), these Italian feminists argue that sexual difference is both ontologically grounded and as yet unrealised. Following Irigaray, they believe that feminism must inscribe femininity in the Symbolic—that is, feminists must create a culture that gives voice to female difference as manifested in the morphology of the female body and in women's ability to reproduce. To create such a culture women must bond with one another—not, however, as sisters (as the egalitarian feminism of the 1970s recommended) but as (symbolic) mothers and daughters. In order to name this relationship, the Italian feminists coined the term *affidamento*, which combines the Italian roots of 'faith', 'loyalty', 'trust' and 'to confide'. *Affidamento*, they claim, is the key to the emancipation of the feminine, and therefore to women's freedom.

The theory of *affidamento* has been taken up enthusiastically in sections of the German feminist movement, which has long been committed to autonomy—not in the liberal sense of individual self-determination, but in the radical and separatist sense of a women-only public sphere. Nevertheless, *affidamento* has been criticised by some theorists in ways that are representative of dominant trends in German feminist thinking. Gudrun-Axeli

Knapp (1991), for example, is not altogether unsympathetic to this approach, but is disturbed by its elitist and separatist tendencies, as manifest in its utter disdain for the politics of equal rights, its effacement of the material conditions of women's oppression and of inequalities between women, and its dubious claim that women are completely outside patriarchal culture and thus not complicit in its crimes. This last point is especially sensitive in Germany, where feminists have recently begun to acknowledge the extent to which women (in some cases their own mothers or aunts) collaborated with Nazism. From a German perspective, the kind of 'tactlessness' (as Knapp puts it; some would say dishonesty) manifest in Irigaray's disclaimer that French women supported the Vichy regime is intolerable (Knapp, 1991:122). While Knapp thinks it important to recognise differences among women as well as between the sexes, she does not want to see hierarchical power relationships established as the privileged form of differentiation. As well as foreclosing the possibility that women might recognise one another as different but equal, this approach also negates various other differences (such as class, ethnicity and sexual orientation) that some German feminists have—perhaps belatedly—begun to confront, after having been strongly criticised for their blindness to such matters.

At the opposite end of the spectrum from this reaffirmation of ontologically grounded difference are American deconstructions of the sex–gender distinction. Here the arguments come from ethnomethodology (Kessler and McKenna, 1978), symbolic interactionism (Ortner and Whitehead, 1981) and discourse analysis (Butler, 1990). According to this view, we are not born male and female (*zweigeschlechtlich*) as Carol Hagemann-White states provocatively (1988). Sexual dimorphism is not biologically given, but is as much a social construct as gender. Sexual difference is thus an identity formed in the context of social interaction or produced by the social discourses that shape our reality, and then retrojected on to the body, irrespective of ambiguities and other possibilities of differentiation.

In presenting the ethnomethodological and symbolic-interactionist case for the social construction of sexual dimorphism, Carol Hagemann-White (1988:226–7) notes a certain resistance to

*While still
emphasizing
diff, don't need
womothinood to.*

such thinking within the former West Germany. This she attributes to the strength of the autonomous women's movement, which generally favours theories of female difference. Meanwhile, a number of German feminist theorists have begun to integrate these American ideas on sexual difference as social construct into their work. For instance, Susanne Günther and Helga Kotthoff (1991) argue that in many cultures alleged differences in male and female speech patterns are by no means as fixed as had previously been assumed, and are related primarily to differences in social status. Since the publication in 1991 of the German translation of *Gender Trouble* (1990), Butler's subversive discourse analysis of sexual difference has also been widely discussed. Her work is seen as particularly valuable in undermining the hegemonic claim by white, middle-class and heterosexual feminists to speak for all women. However, this assimilation of sex to gender is resisted by some German feminists because of its apparent implications for the status of the body. Duden (1993), who has herself drawn attention to how perceptions of the body are historically formed and culturally mediated (1991a), sees in Butler's disembodiment of sexual identity—and its popularity among her students—striking evidence of the loss of an interior sense of the body. Within this theory, the body is clearly seen from outside—that is, as object, infinitely susceptible to manipulation, reconstruction and reinterpretation (Duden, 1993). In this, Butler's body-as-text suggests a new phase in that problematic trajectory of enlightenment which has led away from a lived sense of the body as *Leib* to an externalised view of the body as *Körper*. Given the impossibility of establishing where biology ends and culture begins, and the diversity of women's experience and self-understanding, the theorisation of female subjectivity must remain radically open, according to Schuller (cited in Conrad and Konnertz, 1986:11). Yet as some of the German contributors to the 1993 Butler-controversy (Duden, Lorey, Landweer, Lindemann) have indicated, this project should still incorporate a positive conception of the body, as both a precondition for selfhood and a dimension of it. In my view too, this is essential. Otherwise, feminists will have nothing with which to counter the patriarchal illusion of the autonomous subject but a postmodern textualism that simply radicalises the dissociation of the human from its material basis in a body shaped by ecology and evolution as well as marked by cultural inscriptions.

5

Women and Art: From Aestheticised Femininity to Feminist Aesthetics

'It all began with the hidden woman', writes Maria Kublitz-Kramer (1992:41, my trans.) in her review of German feminist research in literary studies. The referent here is threefold. 'The hidden woman' is all those women whose empirical histories and subjectivities have been rendered invisible by an imagined femininity compounded of patriarchal ideology, male fantasies and traces of archaic myth. She is also all those women writers whose works have been forgotten, suppressed, marginalised, or rendered invisible by the presuppositions and conventions of patriarchal literary history. Finally, and implicitly, 'The Hidden Woman' (*Die verborgene Frau*) is the title of a collection of essays edited by Inge Stephan and Sigrid Weigel (1983), which occupies a significant place in the history of German feminist critiques of imagined femininity and the recovery and rereading of women's writing.

Although the relationship between women and art in the German region was first theorised in the area of literary studies, and above all *Germanistik*, feminist research of a similar nature has been undertaken also by art historians, film theorists and musicologists since the early 1980s. Moreover, this work of recovery, reinterpretation and theoretical reflection has been accompanied by an efflorescence of women's writing, art and film in the context of the women's movement, as well as by lively debates about the possibility and characteristics of a specifically 'feminine', or (as some prefer) 'feminist' aesthetics.

In the interests of brevity and clarity, this chapter focuses on feminist literary theory. Wherever possible, however, I have endeavoured to indicate that German feminist discussions of the women-and-art nexus embrace all areas of creative endeavour, and are frequently conducted on an inter- or transdisciplinary basis.

Figurations of the feminine in patriarchal culture

The critical analysis of patriarchal images of women has become a major component in the German feminist critique of Enlightenment. As well as providing a reference-point in the theorisation of both female subjectivity and feminist ethics and spirituality, it has also been central to discussions of the relationship between women, femininity and art. The first major theoretical contribution was Bovenschen's *Die imaginierte Weiblichkeit* (1979), an influential analysis of cultural stereotypes of femininity and their impact on the self-conception and literary production of writing women.

The historical focus of her study is the eighteenth century, a time when both the image of woman and the lives of real women were being transformed through the emergence of modern bourgeois society. Bovenschen's point of departure is the discrepancy between the paucity of writing women in histories constructed by men, and the abundance of female figures in men's literature. Her analysis of the shift from the early Enlightenment programme of female erudition to the later ideal of female sentiment reveals the systematic nature of this discrepancy. For while there are few literary figurations of the learned woman, the potentially egalitarian programme for enhancing and expanding women's education licensed women themselves to write, at least within the rationalistic and formalistic limits of eighteenth-century poetics. Socially privileged women such as Adelgunde Gottsched, whose husband was a noted German literary reformer and neo-classicist dramatist, duly availed themselves of such opportunities. However, because this programme ran counter to the social requirement that women be confined to an increasingly privatised bourgeois domestic sphere, it was soon suppressed by a new discourse on the complementary characteristics of the sexes. Unlike her erudite but (apparently) aesthetically uninteresting predecessor, the new 'woman of sentiment' appears pre-eminently in the writings of philosophers and littérateurs as image and aesthetic object. As Bovenschen's discussion of texts by Rousseau, Herder, Kant and Schiller indicates, this idealisation of female sensitivity and sentiment had negative implications for both women's right to an intellectual education and their ability to write creatively. The feminisation of culture proclaimed by the discourse of sentiment was accompanied by a critique of normative poetics. This certainly favoured women writers by legitimating new forms of literature, such as the epistolary novel, which drew more on contemporary life than on a knowledge of the classics. However, because this discourse posited women's 'nature' as essentially receptive, their artistic creativity was deemed at best mimetic, and in danger of corruption by too intellectual an education. Women who wrote and published in this context therefore transgressed the dominant ideal of femininity, even where the form and subject of their writing apparently reinforced that ideal, as in Sophie von La Roche's epistolary novel, *Geschichte des Fräuleins von Sternheim*.

In general, Bovenschen tends to stress the all-pervasiveness of imagined femininity. Only in this form, she notes, have women found a place in cultural history: real women have no history— or rather, it remains to be written. In the introductory section of her book, Bovenschen discusses two major influences on representations of the feminine: reduction theories and theories of complementarity. In this context, she analyses Wedekind's Lulu-plays (1895, 1902) as symptomatic of the cultural invisibility of women: Wedekind attempts to undermine current stereotypes of femininity by recourse to the notion of a prior and more 'authentic' female nature, which can nevertheless only appear negatively, namely in Lulu's refusal of the roles that her various lovers expect her to play. Wedekind's Lulu is neither a pseudo-man nor man's other half; in Bovenschen's view, she none the less becomes a model for the twentieth-century construction of woman as 'vamp'.

Here, as in her earlier essay on the witch (1978), Bovenschen sees the discourse on femininity as an ideological construction that disguises the reality of social relations. By shaping women's self-understanding it delimits their possibilities of action and expression, and legitimises their subordination within patriarchal society. But as Inge Stephan (1983a) observes, ideological critique is not the only way of analysing patriarchal images of women in literature. Other feminist approaches include the psychoanalytic, which treats images of women (or, more generally, the 'feminine') as pre-eminently 'male fantasies'; the socio-historical, which finds in female literary figures traces of women's historical reality, subject of course to ideological distortion and male projection; and the mythological, which seeks in such figures residues of a pre-patriarchal or (as Göttner-Abendroth [1980] insists) matriarchal understanding of women as powerful and even divine. While Stephan is sceptical of the matriarchal approach, she accepts the possibility that fragments of an archaic mythic consciousness may well resurface in later texts, and argues in favour of reading images of women in ways which take account, as far as possible, of all four approaches. This eclectic approach is characteristic of a number of essays on literary images of woman in this and later volumes in a series (published by *Das Argument*) on feminist literary studies (e.g. Stephan, 1983b; Weigel, 1983a; Stephan, 1984; Prokop, 1984). More recently, Anna Maria Stuby (1992) has also contributed significantly to the multi-faceted analysis of images of woman by studying historical transformations of the 'water woman' motif from Homer's sirens through to Heiner Müller's ironic recasting of Ophelia as a radical feminist in his play *Hamletmachine* (1984). Drawing on various disciplines and methodologies (notably the structuralism of Lévi-Strauss, Foucauldian discourse analysis, Critical Theory, and systems theory), Stuby tends to support Stephan's view that whatever pre-patriarchal elements might still be discernible in Homer's sirens had been lost by the early nineteenth century. Enlisted by the Church Fathers in their campaign against schismatic and secularising tendencies (which were linked discursively with the threat posed by women's unruly sexual appetite), the water woman was split subsequently into a domesticated mother figure and a demonic vamp, these being the twin encodings of the ambivalent bourgeois discourse of love and marriage. As the discourse of passionate love became progressively 'hysterised' through its association with female madness and death, the water woman was turned into a corpse, as in the many literary and visual representations of Shakespeare's Ophelia around 1900. Overall, the history that Stuby retraces is, by now, familiar: the gradual marginalisation, disempowerment, and dehumanisation of the feminine.

German feminist studies of female literary figures now fill many shelves, and they have been joined since the early 1980s by comparable critiques of imagined femininity in the visual arts and film (e.g., Bischoff et al., 1984; Barta et al., 1987; Lindner et al., 1989; Breitling, 1990, and in *Frauen und Film*, a journal founded in 1974). While the analysis of discrete images of Woman remains important, it is no longer assumed that such representations of femininity constitute a form of false consciousness, veiling an empirical reality which we alone, as late twentieth-century feminist critics and historians, can know objectively. On the contrary, literary and artistic images are seen as elements in the discursive construction of an ambiguous and contradictory socio-historical reality, access to which is mediated by the discourses that construct our own world(s) in the present, and only recently has attention been paid to the wider role of gender in their artistic production and historical reconstructions of it. Examples include the volume edited by Ines Lindner and others (1989) on constructions of masculinity and femininity in art and art history, Elisabeth Bronfen's literary studies of femininity, art and death (1987, 1992), Sigrid Weigel's exploration of the discursive gendering of different social spaces (1990a), and Gabriele Althoff's study of the topos of femininity as art (1991).

Althoff's work provides a particularly good example of a distinctively German feminist approach to imagined femininity. Her analysis of both visual and literary texts from the Renaissance to the late nineteenth-century indicates the close collaboration between literary theorists and art historians in the German-speaking region. Moreover, her deployment of Critical Theory and discourse analysis facilitates that socio-historical contextualising of contemporary concerns which is characteristic of much German feminist theory. Indirectly, Althoff's book constitutes a critical intervention in the debate about feminine aesthetics arising from the German reception of French feminist theory. In brief,

Althoff argues that the association between Woman and art as the subversive Other of patriarchal order and its dominant rationality has a historical index reaching back to the Renaissance. Her analysis focuses on the changing representation of two com- plementary figures—the adulteress and Don Juan—which she identifies as aesthetic crystallisations of this cultural interpretive model. Althoff concludes that the discourse on femininity as art has generally performed a compensatory social function: as an imaginary realm of freedom or disfunctionality, it both negates and stabilises the instrumental rationality of the masculine realm of commerce, politics and professional life. (Dorothea Dornhof [1993] reaches a similar conclusion.) Implicitly, this historical reconstruction casts doubt on the socially transformative potential of the new feminist equation of femininity with an aesthetics of rupture, desire and ambivalence, as proposed by Irigaray and Cixous.

Reading women's texts: rewriting cultural history

In addition to critiquing the existing canon—in which woman figures as sign, but rarely as subject—feminists in the German- speaking region have set about recovering from archives, attics and cellars, lost or forgotten literary, visual and musical texts produced by women. They have also reinterpreted according to new critical criteria those few women's texts already incorporated into the canon. Far from having no history, as Bovenschen asserted in 1979, reflecting the state of literary historiography at that time, it is now evident that women have a rich literary and artistic heritage of their own, even if it cannot be considered wholly separate from the dominant traditions of western culture. On a theoretical level, this work of recovery and reinterpretation has been accompanied by reflections on how women's writing relates both to their historical experience and to the traditional canon, and has given rise to feminist critiques of the mechanisms of canon-formation in general.

Inge Stephan's discussion of images of women thus has its counterpart in 'The Hidden Woman' in Sigrid Weigel's essay (1983b) on the history of women's writing, which argues:

because the impoverished tradition of women's culture is not only a consequence of the meagre cultural production of women but also the result of male norms and attitudes as to what constitutes tradition, any consideration of women's history must necessarily be linked to a critique of existing literary theory and history (Weigel, 1985:60).

The view that to reconstruct women's literary history implies something more radical than simply inserting female authors into a male-dominated canon is common among German feminist literary historians. As Hiltrud Gnüg and Renate Möhrmann (1985) observe in the introduction to their comparative history of women's writing from the Middle Ages to the present—the very first in German—conventional literary history is inappropriate in the case of women's writing, which does not always fit neatly into recognised epochs and styles. Yet women's writing does not constitute a cohesive counter-tradition either, since often it has been produced in relative isolation and with no awareness of female predecessors. Characterised therefore by discontinuities, women's literary history does not lend itself to a narrative of development, which is why Gnüg and Möhrmann opt for an essayistic approach rather than a continuous account.

In introducing the first volume of a similarly essayistic history of women's writing in German, Gisela Brinker-Gabler (1988) also draws attention to the nationalistic and elitist underpinnings of literary historiography as it was constituted as an academic discipline in the mid-nineteenth century. Its dominant narrative is the emergence and consolidation of a national spirit, manifest in the works of exceptional individuals (preferably male), who write in privileged styles and genres. The same processes of national myth-making have been analysed by German feminist art historians like Wenk (1989). By mirroring themselves in 'great artists' and their work, male critics and historians establish a patrilineal progression of cultural production. How can women's work be rendered visible without producing a parallel pantheon (or 'museum', as Weigel [1985:59] puts it), in which the new criteria of inclusion and exclusion are female authorship or feminist consciousness or both? The solution proposed by Brinker-Gabler

(1988:14, my trans.) is an expanded concept of literature as 'social process . . . determined by changing loci and modalities of communication'. From this perspective, there are two key questions for feminist literary and art historians. To what extent could women participate in particular social communication processes? And in what ways might possible differences in the socio-historical formation of women's mentality have created specific limitations and opportunities for women writers and artists, especially with regard to male paradigms and aesthetic norms?

Like Brinker-Gabler, Weigel emphasises the ambivalence of women's position as both involved in and excluded from the male order. Thus she distinguishes women's culture from that of a number of different collective subjects which western culture has also commonly constituted as 'other' (Weigel, 1985:62). Since they do not form a numerical minority, women cannot be considered 'outsiders' in the same sense that Hans Mayer (1982)— who fails to differentiate between patriarchal projections and the historical experience of real women—considers Jews and homosexuals. In patriarchal conditions, women not only learn to see themselves as mirrored in the male gaze, but also reproduce the male order through their domestic labour. In this respect, women's culture does not constitute a separate 'sub-culture' (Weigel, 1985:62). Although the relationship between the sexes can be seen as dialectical, women's sexual bond with men, entailing their complicity with a 'representative of the ruling culture' (ibid.), renders an analogy with Lenin's theory of 'two cultures'— proletarian and bourgeois—similarly inappropriate. Weigel acknowledges that in some regards at least women might seen as the victims of a historical process of colonisation, but argues— against the proponents of matriarchal aesthetics and spirituality— that since all memories of an 'independent pre-patriarchal culture' have by now been erased, women's culture cannot be likened to the 'alien cultures' of more recently colonised peoples either (ibid.:63).

The ambivalence produced by women's complicity and marginality, inclusion and exclusion, necessitates that 'double focus' referred to here by Weigel (1985). Her aim is to focus—as if with a sideways gaze (*'schielender Blick'*)—on the question of women's art and writing in a culture dominated by masculine models (including constructions of femininity), without losing sight of the wider socio-historical processes with which this feminist problematic is connected.

Against this theoretical background, Weigel (ibid.:60ff.) indicates some of the ways in which women writers of the nineteenth and twentieth centuries have sought to express themselves publicly 'in spite of the confinement in the personal and the private'. As Bovenschen observes in her article 'feminine aesthetics' (originally published in 1977), this has been a 'complicated process involving conquering and reclaiming, appropriating and formulating, as well as forgetting and subverting' (1985:47). While resisting the temptation to read all women's writing as necessarily subversive or innovative, Weigel shows how even socially normative texts (like the mid-nineteenth-century novels of Fanny Lewald, which generally conclude with the punishment or renunciation of her wayward heroines) might contain elements of resistance in the transgressive fantasies of their female characters. Weigel reads 'between the lines' and 'against the grain', attending to moments of 'dereflection', where the male mirror of femininity is broken, and of protest, as for example in women's narratives of illness, where the body speaks out against the subjection that cannot be articulated otherwise. Consequently, Weigel indicates that women writers have been less narrowly confined by masculine norms than Bovenschen assumes in *Die imaginierte Weiblichkeit*.

While making gender a central category for analysing work by both men and women, feminist critics have also challenged the code of femininity conventionally used when interpreting women's texts. Marianne Schuller (1990c:103ff.), for example, has argued that the editors of two recent republications of the psychoanalytic writings of Sabine Spielrein (a contemporary and client of both Freud and Jung) have rendered her texts once more invisible by pathologising and aestheticising both them and their author. It has been necessary to dislodge traditional hierarchies of worth in order to revalue previously marginalised forms frequently favoured by women, such as the diary and letter, or domestic arts and crafts like embroidery. But it has been equally important to recover women's work in genres and styles conventionally considered masculine. Dagmar von Hoff (1989), for instance, has analysed a number of plays written by women around 1800, the existence of which had previously been overlooked, largely because it was assumed until recently that drama was a preserve of male writers.

This recovery and rereading of earlier women's texts was concurrent with the emergence of a new women's art and literature in the 1970s and 1980s, which has in turn become the object of feminist analysis. In an interesting redeployment of the critique of images of woman, Gisela Ecker (1994b) has shown, for example, how traditional representations of the mother-and-child motif are subjected to various forms of alienation, dislocation and subversion in the work of contemporary women painters, who thereby produce some different perspectives on motherhood from that conveyed by desexualised and idealised representations of the Madonna and Child.

Feminist investigations of contemporary women's fiction in German are now numerous (see Richter-Schröder, 1986; Brügmann, 1986; Venske, 1988 and Becker, 1992). From a theoretical perspective, the most significant to date is in my view *Die Stimme der Medusa* by Sigrid Weigel (1987a). In 'Double Focus' (1985), Weigel had been concerned to uncover the historical traces of genuine female experience and aspirations in earlier women's writing. Here, however, she proceeds from the Foucauldian premise that experience is pre-formed discursively. Weigel thus highlights the contradictions inherent in the project of an authentic women's literature by showing how recent women's fiction is conditioned by particular cultural models and societal pressures. This is not intended as a condemnation of contemporary women's writing. It arises rather from Weigel's conviction that before a substantial feminist transformation (of literature and society) can occur it is necessary to understand the ways in which both our perceptions and our modes of expression are shaped by contradictory cultural discourses, each of which has its own history. This does not imply, however, that all prior models and historical discourses are simply oppressive. One of the most interesting parts of Weigel's study concerns the rediscovery in the 1980s of the 'pre-feminist' women writers of the 1950s and 1960s. These include the Austrian writers Ingeborg Bachmann (1990) and Marlen

Haushofer (1957, 1958, 1963), whose representations of female impairment, illness and uncertainty can now be reread in the context of psychological analyses of how women's subjectivity is constrained by dominant concepts of femininity and female sexuality.

In addition to restating her earlier critique of canonisation, while conceding that the reconstruction of literary history will result inevitably in new exclusions, Weigel insists that the texts she focuses on serve merely as examples, and could theoretically be replaced by others. In order to shift attention from authorship to modes of writing within the symbolic system of literature, Weigel organises her account around themes and genres (such as subjectivity, the body, autobiography, satire, the return to love, and the recasting of myth) rather than individual writers and works. Focusing on constellations and 'snap-shots' rather than attempting an exhaustive account, Weigel re-presents contemporary women's fiction in all its variety and vitality. She thus refuses to elide the contradictions and dissynchronicities ('*Ungleichzeitig-keiten*') that characterise women's literature by pressing everything into a linear history of development.

Feminine or feminist aesthetics?

The recent recovery, rereading and production of texts by women has been accompanied by lively discussions about the possibility of a distinctively female or feminine aesthetic. As Gisela Ecker (1985b) comments when introducing her collection of texts on this subject—entitled, significantly, *Femin*ist *Aesthetics*—most German-speaking contributors to this topic do not proceed from essentialist or biologistic assumptions, even though the ambiguity of the German term *weiblich* might suggest otherwise. For example, although Bovenschen (1985:36ff.) believes that women should develop 'different aesthetic forms' which embody 'specifically feminine modes of perception', she thinks of these as grounded in women's historical experience of marginalisation rather than in some timeless 'femininity'. Similarly, for Elisabeth Lenk (1985:51, 57) 'feminine aesthetics' does not signal the 'return of typically "feminine" elements of art' (whatever they might be), but is the product of women 'taking command of their fantasies', and learning to mirror themselves in other women rather than in the reifying gaze of men.

Bovenschen, Lenk and others (such as the musicologist Eva Rieger [1985]), all associate the emergence of a 'feminine aesthetics' with the appropriation, subversion and transformation by women of prevailing aesthetic norms. Göttner-Abendroth (1985, 1991b), on the other hand, argues for the development of a completely different aesthetic practice based on the recovery of suppressed matriarchal traditions. Accordingly, her theory is concerned neither with feminine nor feminist aesthetics, but rather with the 'principles of a matriarchal aesthetics'. Whereas modern patriarchal aesthetics is defined as the 'free play of possibilities' within the 'ghetto' of art, matriarchal aesthetics envisages a 'liberating play of realities', directed towards the ultimate 'aestheticisation of society'. Göttner-Abendroth defines matriarchal art as 'neither work nor ware nor fetish', but as an 'energetic process' in which producer, consumer and critic become inseparable, and distinctions between different genres and art forms, theory and praxis, art and life, disappear. Like many artists and theorists of the Romantic and modernist avant-garde, she seeks to undo those processes of differentiation which characterise modern culture and society, and which enabled the aesthetic to acquire a relative autonomy from other areas of social and cultural life, such as religion, politics and ethics. As becomes clear from the 'seasonal cycle' described in the final section of her book, Göttner-Abendroth's model of a matriarchal *Gesamtkunstwerk* (a term coined by Wagner, referring to a work of art unifying all art forms) corresponds to the ritual practices of post-Christian feminist spirituality. This is not 'fiction', but 'magic', the efficacious enactment of myth, directed towards the 'continuation of life as a cycle of rebirths' (Göttner-Abendroth, 1985:81, 83).

This intervention into the feminine aesthetics debate aroused considerable interest in the early 1980s, but has been seen as problematic in a number of ways. Doubts have been raised concerning the legitimacy of postulating a prehistoric matriarchal past as the source of subterranean cultural traditions continuing into the present day. Göttner-Abendroth's assimilation of aesthetics into spirituality leaves no room for the kind of oppositional or subversive art that many feel is necessary, given the current state of the world: to live Utopia now in the ecstasy of the dance might inspire and regenerate both individuals and groups of women, but is unlikely to bring down patriarchy. The history of the avant-garde, which ultimately failed to dismantle the social systemic distinction between art and life, indicates that no attempt to reverse the processes of societal differentiation through the aestheticisation of life can be effected entirely and successfully from within the sphere of the aesthetic. Matriarchal aesthetic practices will be either recuperated to the ghetto of art, or become part of a subcultural life-style within a sector of the women's movement.

By contrast with such visions of an autonomous women's culture of aesthetics and spirituality, Gisela Breitling (1985), herself a practising artist, has argued in favour of what might be called the 'mainstreaming' of women's art. The fact that many contemporary women artists prefer anti-classical materials and forms—such as ready-mades, performance art, video and mixed media—while others attempt to develop a new feminine discourse on and of art, is in Breitling's opinion understandable, for it indicates a response by women to their marginalisation within male-defined norms of aesthetic production. But it is in the long run inadequate, as it involves reinforcing—this time from the feminist side—the gender apartheid of patriarchal culture (Breitling, 1990). Protesting against the banishment of women artists to the 'ghetto of the feminine', Breitling (1985:166) calls instead for a radically new 'universality' in art, beyond the unacknowledged identification of the universal with masculinity.

Discussions of feminine aesthetics in German literary studies have been shaped largely by the reception of French feminist theory as represented by Julia Kristeva, Luce Irigaray and Hélène Cixous, whose work excited considerable interest when it was presented at the first national meeting of German women writers in 1976. Later that year, a number of interviews with and articles by Kristeva, Irigaray, Cixous and also Catherine Clément were published in the journal *alternative*. Subsequently, all the major works of these French theorists—as well as several articles and interviews—have appeared in German translation. The main proponents of the French approach in the FRG are Marianne Schuller and Eva Meyer. Although Meyer's work, for example on the semiotics of the feminine (1983) and the autobiography of writing (1989) is fascinating (if rather inaccessible), her approach is somewhat atypical of the German feminist reception of French feminism. At the risk of oversimplifying, both Meyer and (to a lesser extent) Schuller, *do* French theory in German, whereas most German feminists who take an interest in developments across the western border *engage with* it critically, if not always unsympathetically.

In 'Double Focus', for example, Weigel includes a brief discussion of the concept of *écriture feminine* in Irigaray and Cixous. Weigel is sympathetic to their analysis of the place of the feminine in patriarchal culture, and thinks that Irigaray's strategy of 'traversing' phallocentric discourse in order to undo its systematic suppression of the feminine is a useful adjunct to feminist critique. But she is more sceptical of the project of 'writing the body', and argues that the theory of *écriture feminine* invites a remystification of femininity to the extent that it fails to differentiate clearly enough between patriarchal projections of the feminine, the lived experience of women, and the utopian project of developing new models of subjectivity and creativity (Weigel, 1985:75–80).

In general, Kristeva's model of *écriture feminine* is far less controversial within German feminist theory because it is unambiguously non-essentialist. However, as Weigel (1987a) observes, the particular problems of women as writers are for this very reason secondary to Kristeva's theory of the 'revolution in poetic language'. Indeed, that subversion of the symbolic order of the text by the eruption of suppressed memories of a mother–child symbiosis—which Kristeva reveals in the writings of poets such as Arthur Rimbaud and Stéphane Mallarmé—tends to presuppose male authorship, in so far as such subversions are in her view safe only for those who are well anchored in the Symbolic. This observation also guides Marlis Gerhardt (1986), for whom Virginia Woolf and Gertrude Stein exemplify a different avant-garde, constituted by women writers within modernism who avoid the kind of hermetic language that would simply reinforce their exclusion from the Symbolic. Their writing thus occupies a third position beyond that Oedipal conflict in which the language of literary fathers is negated in the revolt of avant-garde sons. Karin Richter-Schroeder (1986) has also drawn upon Kristeva's analysis of the ambivalent position of women in relation to the symbolic order in order to develop a non-essentialist theory of feminine aesthetics. But whereas Gerhardt shows how modernist women's writing corrects or at least supplements the theory of *écriture feminine*, Richter-Schroeder uses her theoretical model as a critical yardstick. Second-wave German feminist texts like Verena Stefan's *Shedding* (1979) are shown to be at fault because, instead of turning their marginality to advantage by illuminating the repressive effects of the symbolic order in the subject-formation of women, they simply reproduce female suffering.

In a more recent article Richter-Schroeder (1992) reiterates a common German feminist critique of the allegedly ahistorical and biologistic tendencies in the feminine aesthetics of Cixous and Irigaray. According to Gisela Ecker, however, biological reductionism is less common in Irigaray and Cixous (at least up until the mid-1980s) than in some of their followers. In the introduction to *Feminist Aesthetics*, Ecker contends that whereas 'the originators of the discourse about *écriture feminine* perform a brilliant tightrope act which keeps them from falling into blunt essentialism . . . in the hands of their successors these ideas about "woman's voice" sometimes approach prescriptive views of what women's writing should be like' (Ecker, 1985b:18). In another article on post-structuralism and feminist knowledge (1985a), she points out that Cixous, who is widely seen by German feminists as the most problematic of the French theorists, is in fact careful to keep the concept of the feminine open and multiple. Although Cixous' metaphorisation of the female body appears in some respects dependent on the patriarchal code of imagined femininity, Ecker (ibid.:17) considers that the ideological implications of this code might be transcended in Cixous' redeployment of it and in the feminist reception of her texts. On the other hand, if this new version of the topos of femininity as art is not linked to more social and political strategies of feminist transformation, it could end up performing the same kind of merely compensatory function that (according to Althoff [1991] and Dornhof [1993]) earlier versions have.

Despite her qualified defence of these French models of *écriture feminine* against accusations of biologism, Ecker (1985b:21) argues that the constant danger of engendering new fixed identities or resurrecting old ones obliges us 'to pursue not a "feminine" but a "feminist" aesthetics'. It should be non-prescriptive on questions of style, but 'critical of traditional assumptions'; and it should take into account 'the complications of subjectivity' and the varying historical contexts in which women's texts have been produced and received. In Ecker's assessment, the new universality in art called for by Breitling represents a 'future stage which cannot be achieved without going through the equally radical introduction of gender into hitherto "unaffected" fields' (ibid.:22). Yet Breitling's ideal of universality may itself be a false Utopia. Given the internal differentiation of the feminist public sphere, and the fact that women also participate in other kinds of groupings within the polymorphous culture of postmodernity, it is perhaps more important to acknowledge the variety of aesthetic possibilities and associated political strategies currently being explored by women as writers, artists, musicians and film-makers, than to judge them according to the normative criteria of either the feminine or the universal.

6

Immanence and Difference: Feminist Ethics and Spirituality

Feminine or feminist ethics?

Questions of value are intrinsic to any feminist enquiry that retains its connection with the political project of women's emancipation. Feminism necessarily incorporates ethical reflection on the nature and preconditions of the good life for women, whether in terms of equal rights, self-determination or the cultivation of difference. Moreover, as a critique of patriarchy, feminism challenges the dominant values and norms in western civilisation. Feminist ethics is distinguished by weaker and stronger forms of this challenge. Arguments in favour of abortion on demand, for example, or against pornography, rape, domestic violence and sexual harassment, rely heavily on the enlightenment discourse on human rights. The extension of such ethical principles to women undoubtedly challenges the prevailing double standard in society. It also produces significant shifts in definition and application, as when feminists claim that the right to freedom from bodily harm implies the right to terminate an unwanted pregnancy, or that pornography silences women by humiliating and objectifying them, thus infringing their right to free speech. Clearly, the discourse of enlightenment has proven strategically useful to feminists in such cases. Some feminists go further in advocating a radical overhaul of all existing hierarchies of value, including the Enlightenment legacy itself. It is this feminist 'transvaluation of all values', as the first-wave German feminist Helene Stöcker (echoing Nietzsche's *Umwertung aller Werte*) termed her 'New Ethics' in 1905 (Brick, 1992:165), that concerns us here.

The aspiration to develop a new ethics—in the interests not just of women's emancipation but of society generally—has been equally important in second-wave German feminism. Since the early 1970s a distinctively feminist (or, as some would have it, feminine) ethics has emerged in the FRG as a result of feminist engagement with problems of militarism, nuclear energy, environmental destruction, genetic engineering, reproductive technology and, most recently, racism. Despite broad agreement as to the substance of this new ethics, feminists disagree as to how such values as non-violence, recognition of difference, acceptance of ecological limits and respect for life should be theoretically grounded. Aware of the history and ideological function of the association between Woman, peaceableness, and nature, and between sexual and racial Otherness, few feminist theorists claim that an intrinsically female morality induces women to support pacifism, environmentalism or anti-racism. Some have argued, however, that the social conditioning of women (especially into motherhood) endows them with a different moral sense, which makes them specially responsible for peace, nature and even the future of humanity. Margarete Mitscherlich (1987), for example, thinks that unless the 'future is feminine' there will be no future. Having internalised so-called motherly characteristics, women are in her view predestined to promote the values of compassion, understanding and tolerance in a world dominated by masculine prejudice, paranoia and violence (Mitscherlich, 1983a:183). Contributors to a volume published a year after the Chernobyl nuclear disaster likewise call upon women as actual or potential mothers to counter the catastrophic values and practices of the prevailing technopatriarchy, to use a term coined by Mies, before it is too late (Gambaroff et al., 1986).

Such critics emphasise the importance of eliminating that sexual division of labour that fosters the male proclivity for aggression and ecological vandalism (Mitscherlich, 1987:19–20; Stopczyk, 1986:197). But their stress on the importance of aptitudes and attitudes acquired by women through their child-care responsi-

*against
idealized
motherhood(?)*

ɔeems to be at odds with this socially transformative
..ibition. Moreover, as Herrad Schenk (1983:104–5) points out in
her book on feminism and pacifism, the identification of motherhood with 'motherliness' is a suspiciously bourgeois legacy.
Historically, the ethics of mothering have been ambivalent:
mothers have more often sent their sons to war than intervened
in the interests of peace. Given what the American historian
Claudia Koonz (1987) has revealed about mothers in the Nazi
Fatherland, many German feminists are wary of the idealisation
of 'motherliness' implicit in Mitscherlich's model of a feminised
morality. For these reasons, Schenk argues that a feminist ethics
of non-violence should be based on analyses of the structural
connections between militarism, male violence and the patriarchal
domination of women, and not on women's allegedly motherly
characteristics or child-care responsibilities. Similarly, German
ecological feminists generally do not appeal to women's supposedly intrinsic closeness to nature, but argue instead in terms of
structural connections between the domination of nature and the
oppression of women (for example, Bennholdt-Thomsen, 1987),
and (in the case of Maria Mies) the exploitation of colonised
peoples (Mies and Shiva, 1993).

The case against a higher female morality has been put most
forcibly in the FRG by Christina Thürmer-Rohr (1991). Like Schenk,
she thinks that the values and norms conventionally attributed to
women are inseparable from the traditional sexual division of
labour. Historically, feminine gentleness, humility and consideration for others have not constituted an alternative to masculine
aggression and hubris; on the contrary, they have enabled women
to support and affirm the destructive exploits of their menfolk.
What is required now is not a reaffirmation of feminine morality
but a rejection of that male-dominated civilisation which women
have sustained for too long in their capacity as handmaidens,
housewives and mothers. By relinquishing old identities and
certainties, and resisting the temptation to repeat men's mistakes
by remaking the world in their own image, women should accept
their existential homelessness. They can then turn 'vagabonds' in
the name of a truth which is almost too hard to bear (namely,
women's historical complicity in our currently dire situation) and

in the interests of the life which still survives the past ravages and ongoing onslaughts of an institutionalised form of male violence.

Although Thürmer-Rohr does not refer directly here to Carol Gilligan's psychological work, one context for the essays she wrote between 1983 and 1987 is the lively discussion that followed the German publication in 1984 of Gilligan's *In a Different Voice* (1982). Gilligan argues that differences in ethical outlook between men and women are related to differences in male and female identity-formation. Drawing on Nancy Chodorow's theory of the consequences of the female monopoly on child care (1978), Gilligan contends that the little boy's perception of self as opposed to the (M)Other creates a preoccupation with autonomy and a generally more abstract approach to moral questions. Girls, on the other hand, perceive themselves as similar to and connected with the (M)Other; consequently, they develop a more relational and contextual ethical outlook, valorising care and responsibility for others over allegedly universal principles of right and wrong. While Gilligan's book sheds new light on how and why, in certain contexts, women might develop different values and norms from men, it was criticised in the FRG (for example, by Haug, 1984) for failing to account for the socio-historical genesis and ideological function of both the masculine and feminine modes of moral discourse Gilligan encountered in her research. Others, however, have drawn on Gilligan's work constructively in formulating feminist critiques of androcentric ethics. Andrea Maihofer (1992) finds Gilligan's work useful in disclosing the male bias inherent in conceptions of the sovereign self, and in enabling a critique of that moral abstraction and philosophical universalism which is blind to the particularity of situation and the possibility of a plurality of rationalities. This transposition of Gilligan's moral dualism into feminist critique involves taking sides with the other voice—and transforming it into a social praxis—in ways that Gilligan (who stresses the complementarity of masculine and feminine ethics) tends not to do. Mechthild Rumpf (1989), who notes similarities between Chodorow's research and Max Horkheimer's theory that memories of early mother–child symbiosis form the basis of moral feeling, also observes that the sexual asymmetry from which this alleged difference in ethical outlook arises will merely be maintained unless the other voice becomes available to men as well as women (Rumpf, 1992).

Significantly, reconsiderations of earlier feminist goals often accompany the critique of patriarchal and androcentric values. Claudia von Werlhof (1986:9, my trans.) was prompted by the Chernobyl disaster to ask: 'Do we still want to go ever further in the direction of "modernity", "emancipation", "equal rights" and progress, despite Chernobyl? And if not, then where do we want to go, where can we go?' Genetic engineering also brings out conflicts in feminist ethics. Maria Mies (1992) argues that the defence of bio-technological progress on the grounds that it promises to enhance women's reproductive autonomy (and allows them to freely dispose of their 'reproductive material' for profit) discloses a fundamentally flawed conception of self-determination. For the price of such autonomy is the 'heteronymy' of part of the self, the body, which is reduced to the same object-status as non-human nature in becoming a 'store-house for spare-parts and raw materials' (ibid.:129ff., my trans.). Against this model of emancipation as self-mutilation, Mies argues for a new ethos of interconnectedness, linking mind and body, mother and embryo, individuals and communities, and (implicitly) human and non-human nature.

Other German feminist theorists share her valorisation of human bodiliness and human embeddedness in social and ecological networks. Alongside such affirmations of immanence, however, a new 'ethics of difference' is now being developed in German feminism. Both orientations reject abstract universalism in advocating a revalorisation of the particular. However, where immanence is the key term in ecological feminist ethics, 'difference' is central to the postmodernist feminist ethics theorised by Young (1990), Yeatman (1990) and Kristeva (1991). Believing that postmodernism leads only to *in*difference (and hence is incompatible with substantive values, let alone feminist activism), German feminists have tended to view it with suspicion. But Gisela Ecker (1993) argues that postmodernist ethics provides the theoretical basis for an acceptance of heterogeneity and respect for the irreconcilable that are especially necessary in today's culturally and ethnically diverse societies (and not least in Germany, with its history of genocidal intolerance of difference and its current resurgence of racial violence).

Feminist 'liberation theology' and the 'theology of embodiment'

A diverse body of feminist theological writing—frequently in dialogue with secular feminist ethics—has appeared in German over the past decade. Although recent publications include Jewish and Islamic perspectives (Pissarek-Huderlist and Schottroff, 1991; Jost and Kubera, 1991), German feminist theology is overwhelmingly Christian—Lutheran or Roman Catholic—in background. However, it is strongly ecumenical in orientation, and draws on feminist theology from the Netherlands (Halkes, 1980) and the United States (for example, Reuter, 1983; Schüssler-Fiorenza, 1984; Plaskow, 1990), as well as on Latin American liberation theology (for example, Boff, 1985). German feminist theologians have also had to engage with their own historical legacy, especially with regard to anti-Semitic tendencies in German theological traditions, and the widespread collaboration of both the Catholic and Lutheran Churches with the Nazi state. To some extent, this self-scrutiny has been forced on them from outside, above all by the accusations of anti-Judaism levelled at their work by the American Jewish feminist theologian, Susannah Heschel (1987, 1988, 1993). The question of anti-Semitism and anti-Judaism in German feminist theology and spirituality is the subject of the volumes edited by Schaumberger (1987) and Siegele-Wenschkewitz (1988), as well as numerous contributions to the feminist journal of religion, *Schlangenbrut*, and the magazine of liberal Christian thought, *Publik-Forum*.

The Latin *religio* means to 'bind', 'commit oneself', or 'reconnect'. A valorisation of relationship and responsibility is therefore common to both secular and religiously based feminist ethics. German feminist theologians are highly critical of the individualist and hierarchical distortion of the principle of *religio* within traditional Christian teaching and practice, where the impulse to reconnect is limited to the relationship between a privatised believer and an all-powerful, transcendental and implicitly male God (mediated, in the case of Catholicism, by a hierarchically structured and entirely male-dominated Church). The concomitant valorisation of obedience and quietism is seen as having made possible the complicity of the churches with the Nazi regime. Some German feminists also have problems with the fact that although the bond between God and believer may be celebrated sensually (especially within the Catholic Church), it is meant to serve the transcendence of the flesh and is therefore forged at the cost of the body. Since women have generally been regarded as more carnal than men, 'male-stream' Christianity has been profoundly misogynist at times. Examples range from murderous witch-hunts to various discriminatory practices, of which the most obvious is the restriction of entry to the Roman Catholic priesthood to celibate men. Because the stigmatisation of the flesh has been linked frequently with theological disdain for the entire material dimension of life, the churches have only recently begun to oppose the destruction of the ecological basis of human existence.

German feminist theologians call for a radical expansion of the principle of reconnection and commitment. This involves an active solidarity with the oppressed, especially (but not exclusively) with other women throughout the world. It also involves an affirmation of the body, and a commitment to the flourishing of life on earth as God's Creation, of which, as embodied beings, we are a part, and upon which our well-being and freedom depends. New forms of worship are needed to communicate this more worldly understanding of the Christian message, and new ways must be found to reconnect religious faith with everyday life. Feminist liberation theology is about more than anti-patriarchal efforts to secure the ordination of women. As Christine Schaumberger (1991:15, my trans.) writes, recalling a discussion between Adrienne Rich and Audre Lorde, 'it is about every moment of our lives'.

Recent publications attest to the vitality and variety of German feminist liberation theology (Schaumberger and Schottroff, 1988, 1992; Jost and Kubera, 1991; Schulenburg, 1993). The Lutheran theologian Dorothee Sölle is perhaps the most prominent among the socially and politically engaged contributors to these discussions. As she puts it in the title of her 1992 book, her materialist-feminist transvaluation of male-stream theology affirms every person's right to 'a different happiness'—different, that is, from both the individualist pleasures purveyed by consumer capitalism, and the other-worldly redemption promised by transcendental Christianity. It is the right to a self-determined life of work and love, a life free of oppression and exploitation, lived in solidarity with others. Sölle grounds this right in a concept of God as process. The question is no longer whether God exists, but how S/He is realised, here and now in those individual and collective acts of human compassion and justice, which ultimately will build God's City on earth in the form of a world where all men and women can live in peace and freedom. The story of Christ's crucifixion acquires a new immediacy within this politicised theology of immanence. In each and every act of cruelty, exploitation and oppression Christ is crucified again and again; only when such acts (and the social structures that promote or condone them) end, will His resurrection be complete.

Sölle therefore calls for a thorough-going politicisation of the key categories of compassion, guilt, atonement and forgiveness, and for a de-privatisation of prayer. Against the irresponsible infantilism of the patriarchal concept of an all-powerful and autonomous 'Heavenly Daddy', she argues that God depends upon human ears, eyes and hands to perceive wrong and to endeavour to right it. We should therefore face up to our responsibility for creating a better world in co-operation with God, instead of expecting to be the passive recipients of His grace through miraculous intervention. Above all we should acknowledge our individual and collective complicity in the oppression and exploitation of others, both locally and globally. Addressing West German feminists in particular, Sölle contends (1991b:70–1) that the white middle-class women's movement has cultivated personal self-realisation at the expense of solidarity with the less privileged, especially Third World women and their communities.

Das Recht auf ein anderes Glück concludes with a 1978 essay which, recalling God's change of heart after the Flood, advises us to make peace with the earth instead of continuing to worship the destructive God of technological progress and capital accumulation (Sölle, 1992:137–40). She deals with this ecological concern at greater length in *To Love and to Work: A Theology of Creation* (1984), where in the course of affirming the sanctity of the earth, the connectedness of all living things, and the reciprocity of humanity and God as 'co-creators', she delineates a theology of the living body. Characteristic of her political orientation, this is inscribed within (and subordinated to) that 'theology of liberation' which began with the exodus of the Jewish people from slavery in Egypt.

By contrast, the project of developing an ecologically oriented feminist theology of embodiment is central to the work of another Lutheran theologian, Elisabeth Moltmann-Wendel (1994), who initiated and has contributed prolifically to feminist theology in the FRG (see Pissarek-Huderlist and Schottroff, 1991; other contributors to the German discussion of ecological feminist theology and the theology of embodiment include Schottroff, 1986, 1987; and Grossmann, 1987). Moltmann-Wendel's theology, like that of Sölle, is highly christological (that is, centred on the reinterpretation of Christ's message and ministry). But whereas for Sölle the key narrative of Jesus's ministry is that of the Good Samaritan, Moltmann-Wendel focuses on Christ's acts of bodily healing, and in particular on the lesser-known story of the bleeding woman, whose womb was healed after twelve years when she touched Jesus's gown, received his blessing, and was thus restored finally to her community (Mark 5: 24–34). Moltmann-Wendel is one of those German feminist theologians accused of anti-Judaism for allegedly trying to save Christianity for feminism by painting a negative picture of first-century Jewish culture (Heschel, 1988:79). Not surprisingly, therefore, she is careful to locate Christ's positive attitude towards women and the body within holistic Jewish traditions that were lost to institutionalised Christianity when it came under the baleful influence of Hellenistic dualism and especially Stoic sexual ethics (Moltmann-Wendel, 1994:42). But she also relates Jesus's healing ministry to the uniquely Christian mystery of the Incarnation, the key revelation of which is that God is immanent in the body, as in all of Creation. Human beings thus participate in the Divine to the extent that, like Jesus, they are born of women as creatures of flesh and blood. God and humanity, nature and society, earth and cosmos meet in the body. It is thus a source of wisdom that must be heeded, and a divine energy that can be tapped, as it was by the woman who touched Christ's gown and thereby was restored to wholeness. Illness, ageing and certain specifically female experiences—notably pregnancy and giving birth—could be particularly important in the vital project of learning to think with the body, as proposed for example by Annegret Stopczyk (1991).

This theology of embodiment is panentheistic in so far as it imagines God as being at once beyond and within the material universe. The Crucifixion and Resurrection acquire new significance as metaphors for the dissolution of bound matter and energy in the death of the individual, which then provides the basis for the generation of new life. While Sölle wants worship politicised, Moltmann-Wendel calls for its energisation in ways that not only involve and affirm the body but also cultivate a heightened concern for the well-being of those made to suffer in and on account of their embodied difference from the white male norm: women, the sick, the aged, gays, lesbians and people of colour (Moltmann-Wendel, 1994:103). The theology of embodiment 'mistrusts all self-made fantasies of the beyond' (ibid.:104) in its commitment to the restoration of the ecological basis of human life on earth. For, as Moltmann-Wendel (ibid.:xi) remarks in her introduction, liberation occurs not in the beyond but 'in the body'.

This burgeoning of feminist theology has made little impact so far on the Church in Germany, and is only now beginning to influence the teaching and research programmes of theological faculties and colleges (although less so in Roman Catholic institutions, where ordained priests are generally appointed to professorships). Some Protestant feminist theologians, such as Elga Sorge (1986) and Jutta Voss (1988), have actually lost their teaching posts, probably, although not officially, on account of their unorthodox interpretations of the Bible. Unlike their North American counterparts, who campaigned for the ordination of women, German feminists have generally not sought power within the existing structures of the Catholic Church. Andrea Schulenburg (1993:223–4) sees more hope for change in a rebellion at the margins, effected by the creation of 'women church' at the interface between the autonomous feminist movement and the official Church (which in the FRG is maintained by a tax levied by the State). Confronted by the intransigence of institutionalised Christianity and the pervasive androcentrism of its dominant traditions, many religious-minded feminists have abandoned the Church altogether and sought to develop a new 'post-Christian' form of spirituality, frequently drawing on ancient matriarchal images and practices.

The return of the Goddess: Gaian ethics

The foremost German theorist of 'matriarchal spirituality' during the 1980s was Heide Göttner-Abendroth. She reread the Indo-European myths; pieced together the fragmentary and ambiguous archeological record; drew upon and overturned earlier conservative and androcentric theories of matriarchy (notably Johann Jakob Bachofen's *Das Mutterrecht* of 1861); and looked for supporting evidence in ethnological research on the premodern cultures of East Asia, Indonesia and Oceania (Göttner-Abendroth 1991a). Out of all this she has constructed the model—presented in *Die Göttin und ihr Heros* (1980) and *The Dancing Goddess* (1991b)— of a matrilineal, matrifocal, gynocratic, Goddess-worshipping and largely agrarian culture, which was destroyed by those patriarchal civilisations that subsequently arose throughout the Middle East, the Indian subcontinent and Europe. Göttner-Abendroth's controversial theory of matriarchal spirituality seeks to further the feminist transvaluation of patriarchal values by articulating a new, utopian, enlightened mythology. This implies the self-conscious deployment of mythical narratives, symbols and ritual action as a mode of interpreting and being in the world which is at once spiritually regenerative and politically transformative (Göttner-Abendroth, 1989:21–35.). Her interest in the distant matriarchal past is neither merely historical nor entirely ahistorical. Like most contemporary feminist theorists of matriarchy, she does not propose that we endeavour to return to a lost prehistoric world (whose existence in the past remains hypothetical). Instead, she argues for the selective and playful reappropriation of matriarchal forms and values in accordance with present perceptions and

purposes, and above all as a way of resisting the cultural totali-
tarianism of patriarchal society (ibid.:63). In this spirit, she founded
in 1986 the 'Academy and Coven for Critical Matriarchal Research
and Experience' (*Hagia*), which, as its name suggests, aspired to
be a centre not just of learning but also of spiritual practice.

During the 1980s Göttner-Abendroth's theory of matriarchy
excited considerable interest among German feminist theologians;
much of it was critical (Wacker, 1987b, 1988b; Susanne Heine,
1988), but some was sympathetic. The matriarchal approach
inaugurated a significant third stream within German feminist
theology, in the form of research into the suppressed goddesses
of the Old Testament (Weiler, 1984, 1989) and reinterpretations
of both the Virgin Mary (Mulack, 1984) and Jesus Christ (Sorge,
1986; Mulack, 1987) as latter-day embodiments of 'the Goddess
and her hero'. Göttner-Abendroth's work also contributed to the
development of post-Christian forms of feminist spirituality in the
FRG, although more recently she has had less influence than the
American radical feminist Mary Daly (1973, 1978 and 1984) the
'the*a*logian' Carol Christ (1987), the 'new witch' Starhawk (1982,
1987 and 1989), and the popularist German writers and prac-
titioners of feminist spirituality, Luisa Francia (1989) and Ute
Schiran (1988).

German feminist theorists, especially those working in academia, tend to view the women's spirituality movement with
disdain, suspicion, alarm and sometimes even hostility. Because
it values subjective spiritual experience, it is deemed apolitical
and romantic; in treating the body and nature as sacred, it is
accused of tying women to their reproductive function; in seeking
inspiration from the past and other cultures, it is seen as
anachronistic and anti-modern; and because some proto-fascists
and contemporary neo-Nazis are also interested in pre-Judaeo-
Christian spirituality (especially of the Germanic variety) spiritual
feminists are tainted by association (Wagner-Hasel, 1991, 1993;
Kliewer, 1992; Scherzberg, 1992). However, the more differentiated
and sympathetic views of Donate Pahnke (1989, 1990, 1992) and
Hanna Lauterbach (1993) indicate that some are beginning to
take more seriously the philosophical, religious and ethical
challenge of post-Christian feminist spirituality.

Both matriarchal and post-Christian feminist spirituality are centred around the symbolism of the Great Goddess. This too has drawn charges of anti-Semitism, in that it is sometimes claimed, especially by proponents of a matriarchal perspective, that the early Hebrews destroyed the Goddess (Heschel, 1988:88ff.) As Marie-Theres Wacker (1987b; 1988b) has shown, this claim is not only inflammatory, especially in a German context, but also simplistic and ahistorical. This debate has prompted some German feminists to revise their earlier assumptions about Judaism (Weiler, 1987) and others to clarify the nature of their critique (for example, Mulack, 1993). Within more recent discussions of post-Christian feminist spirituality, at least on an academic level, statements of a potentially anti-Semitic kind are scrupulously avoided.

Contemporary goddess-worship is not simply monotheism with a female face. In the spirit of Göttner-Abendroth's enlightened mythology, the Goddess is freely acknowledged as a metaphor for an impersonal force which is identical with rather than beyond the physical universe. Unlike Moltmann-Wendel's panentheistic God, the Goddess is not an external Creator, but a way of imaging that animating and self-generative energy which flows through all things and is the principle of their interconnection (Lauterbach, 1993). Because the Divine is one with the material universe, symbolism is a matter of personal or collective choice; in this sense, feminist spirituality is profoundly anti-fundamentalist. The importance of the Goddess to feminists in industrialised countries is largely cultural and psychological: in a culture that traditionally anthropomorphises the Divine in the figure of an implicitly masculine God, there is much to be gained for women in imaging the Divine in female form (Pahnke, 1992:221). This imaging also entails the risk that cultural stereotypes of femininity will be echoed and endorsed in the figure of the Goddess. According to Pahnke, however, this risk is guarded against within contemporary feminist spirituality, where the image of the Goddess—whether accompanied or not by a male sidekick in the guise of hero or subordinate god—unifies and affirms conventionally dichotomised aspects of femininity, as well as incorporating certain masculine attributes, such as order and form. This is certainly no mere fertility goddess. In fact, Pahnke claims that the 'new witches' (unlike the avatars of New Age spirituality) have become increasingly critical of gender stereotypes, and generally favour the assumption that all so-called secondary sexual characteristics are culturally produced (ibid.:121). This might be a good reason for dissolving the fixed image of the Divine into something more protean and less gendered than the Goddess (as proposed by Andrea Schulenburg, 1993:96ff.), which would also have the advantage of overcoming the residual anthropocentrism inherited by feminist spirituality from Judaism and Christianity.

The Goddess is frequently said to be, in another Nietzschean phrase, 'beyond good and evil'. This does not make feminist spirituality unethical, but it certainly implies that the vagaries of physical existence—notably, sexuality, illness and death—are no longer connected with the idea of original sin (Pfäfflin, 1988:154). Because the Goddess differs from the God of patriarchal monotheism in not being a personal deity, she is not the locus of an authoritarian Divine will, and neither rewards nor punishes individual human actions. Yet because the Goddess is identified with the interconnected self-unfolding of all living things, feminist spirituality respects difference and self-determination, at least where this does not threaten the existence of the whole. In general, the ethics of feminist spirituality are concerned more with the consequences of actions than with their ultimate grounds, as is implied in maxims like 'everything that you do returns to you threefold', and 'where you take, you must also give' (Pahnke, 1992:258, my trans.). Above all, this thealogy of immanence gives rise to what Pahnke has identified as a pre-eminently ecological ethics. The call to live within the limits of ecological sustainability is no longer just a survivalist imperative, but acquires the aura of a sacred duty.

In post-Christian feminist spirituality, accommodation to the rhythms of nature is practised in symbolic forms like seasonal celebrations, lunar rituals and rites of passage. However, ritual is not necessarily seen as adequate in itself. Whereas New Age spirituality collapses the political into the personal, in feminist spirituality individuals and groups are often encouraged to act upon their spiritual insights in the public arena, rather than retaining them for private consumption: hence the ethical maxim of 'taking responsibility for one's visions' (Pahnke, 1990:13, my trans.). Moreover, accommodation to Gaia's laws can be successful only if these are understood. New witches emphasise the value of dreams, intuitions, and imagination—and also traditional knowledges (like herbalism, astrology, Tarot)—as a source of insight and understanding. But these practices are not always coupled with a hostility to science, especially post-mechanistic and self-critical science (Jansen, 1984). Göttner-Abendroth (1988:34) even prefigures an alliance of science and feminist spirituality as two aspects of a new practice of healing required by our present ecological crisis. In light of mutual suspicions, which are perhaps particularly strong in the FRG, it is hardly surprising that such an alliance has not yet appeared.

German critics of matriarchal and post-Christian feminist spirituality often point out that the affirmation of a community of fate between women and nature has proven dangerous, most notably in the Nazi era. There it was assimilated into a eugenically-oriented cult of motherhood, under which some women were declared breeding machines while others were forcibly sterilised or murdered outright (Kliewer, 1987). While it is certainly important to heed this warning, such negative examples should not blind feminists to the even greater danger today of failing to affirm the 'community of fate' between humanity and the earth. In this respect, the main problem with feminist spirituality is not its emphasis on human embodiment and embeddedness in a wider ecology but rather the possibility that such concerns will be seen as women's business only, and marginal at that—thus leaving the men (and increasingly women) of state, science and industry to continue incorrigibly in their old, objectifying and exploitative ways. This danger is greatest where feminist spirituality is conceived as a separatist venture, tapping into an allegedly ancient tradition of women's wisdom, unbroken and untainted by patriarchal civilisation. This tendency appears to have been quite strong in some sectors of the autonomous women's movement in the FRG. In this context, the shift away from essentialist and gynocentric positions within feminist spirituality registered recently by Donate Pahnke (1992:221) is an encouraging sign.

7

Responsibility and Action

Victims or agents?

In 1791 Theodor Gottlieb von Hippel declared that it was in the interests of women (who at that time were minors before the law) to consider themselves—and to be considered—responsible for their own actions; furthermore, that women had to fight their own battles, because men neither could nor should do this for them. Unfortunately, women have not always heeded this important advice.

To expose and analyse patriarchy was the central project of German feminism in the 1970s. It became evident that women lived in a society that was not only hostile, exploitative and alien but also marginalised them to such an extent that they found it virtually impossible to make their influence felt. This emphasis on oppression was appropriate at a time when women were superficially integrated into society. Nominally, they had access to education, all kinds of employment, birth control, and equality before the law; the double standard of morality was also under review. As a result, their grievances were becoming harder to perceive and voice. But feminists' emphasis on marginalisation and grievance coincided with their retreat from mainstream society into a separatist ghetto. Women came to perceive themselves as the innocent and helpless victims of patriarchy, good by nature but powerless to act. Three main events helped change the direction of German feminism. When the fight for more liberal abortion laws was lost in 1975, women began to understand that they needed representation in parliament and the courts if change was to be achieved. Then, after the Chernobyl 'accident' in 1986, they became aware of the need to change the unecological orientations and practices of mainstream society, East and West, before it was too late. And finally, after the fall of the Berlin wall, the unification of East and West Germany, and the accompanying revival of right-wing extremism, women realised that Germans (themselves included) had not come to terms with their national socialist past.

The first to broach the question of women's responsibility was Frigga Haug (1980), who challenged the conceptions of both the good woman and the woman as victim. Women, she argues, are by no means perfect, but often severely deformed by their socialisation within patriarchy. Unless they do something about this they will be unable to take up those new opportunities which emancipation offers them. The study of patriarchy needs to be combined with group therapeutic activity, with the women's movement providing support during the difficult period of readjustment. Haug's cautious article aroused a storm of protest in feminist circles by pointing out that to present women simply as victims of their oppression was not only misleading but also disempowering.

In 1984 Claudia Honegger and Bettina Heintz edited an important collection of essays entitled *Listen der Ohnmacht* ('ruses of the powerless'), which revealed that women never just passively endured the stereotypes and restrictions imposed on them, but also used them to achieve their own ends. Thus the reputed sickliness or frigidity of women allowed them to withdraw, if they so desired, from their housewifely or marital and reproductive duties. Within the parameters set by their circumstances, women had always been rebellious and resourceful.

Christina Thürmer-Rohr's book *Vagabonding*, which was published in German in 1987 in response to the Chernobyl disaster, is a passionate plea to women to face up to the fact 'that men have made a mess of the earth and that women either could not stop it, or didn't notice, or trustingly approved, or resourcefully supported it' (Thürmer-Rohr, 1991:52).

To make amends, women are morally obliged to do three things: they must expose the culture of masculinity, examine their own motives for supporting or not resisting it, and recognise that because they themselves are deeply infected by it they need to change radically. The dominance of masculine culture was made possible by women's unquestioning acceptance of it. It is therefore not surprising that Nazi textbooks produced for little girls, like the one Thürmer-Rohr herself used at school, were devoted almost entirely to arousing admiration for the soldierly and heroic man.

But social conditioning is not the only problem. By co-operating with masculine culture, women have gained spurious advantages, such as peace and quiet in something they could call home, even though it was only a refuge in an alien world. It is consequently important that women should learn to accept homelessness as their true state of being. Furthermore, they should allow themselves to hate productively by opposing passionately and unremittingly everything that they believe to be wrong. Christ's Sermon on the Mount offers a political philosophy for men which throughout history has been abused in order to keep quiet the powerless, prominent among whom are women and the poor. As such, it must be rejected. Peace and quiet cannot be desirable values if ultimately they prevent war against oppression.

Like Haug, Thürmer-Rohr too makes much of the deformations suffered by women in masculine culture, and most noticeably in the realm of morality. Women have been taught to believe that goodness is equivalent to doing no harm, that their purpose in life is to ameliorate male vices, thus preventing the collapse of a culture that otherwise would be self-destructive. They have also been made to believe that theirs is a natural goodness which emanates from a way of being that is unrelated to responsible decision-making. But that putatively natural goodness which women have expressed historically in the form of passive acquiescence cannot possibly solve the problems of our nuclear age.

In much the same way, utopian ideals must be abandoned. Communist hopes for a brighter future (as expressed for example by Ernst Bloch) have served among other things to justify an appalling present. Romantic nostalgia for the past will similarly distract women from their present responsibilities. The present, for Thürmer-Rohr, is that stretch of time over which we still have some control, so that things can be altered, brought about and prevented. The present is our only legacy; there are no alternatives to which we can escape. Thürmer-Rohr insists that the only justifiable approach to western society as currently constituted is resistance; everything in it is questionable, and therefore should be questioned, especially the ideal of love. Referring to her own father's war-time letters from the battlefield, she points out how often our society has intermingled love with lies.

In assuming responsibility for both their own lives and the state of the world, women must acknowledge their own fallibility, if not guilt. However restricted our lives may be, we all make choices which can be right or wrong, good or bad. Since helplessness does not exempt us, it is in our best interests to have the ability to act as we see fit. This involves coming to understand what has caused our acquired helplessness, and seeking opportunities to exert power appropriately and effectively.

Christina Thürmer-Rohr never disputes the claim that patriarchy is the ultimate source of evil. Since women's guilt arises from complicity and inaction, the solution is a total boycott of the masculine system. These axioms, however, have been called into question. Though Thürmer-Rohr's point of departure is her personal experience of the Nazi past, she does not examine it in any detail because she believes in focusing on the present. It took the unification of Germany in 1990—and its consequent upsurge of racist unrest—to direct feminist attention to the period of national socialism. A co-editor of the most controversial collection of essays on this topic, Lerke Gravenhorst, begins by confessing that both her parents were Nazis (Gravenhorst and Tatschmurat, 1990).

Recent debate about the part played by women in national socialism is by no means the first time that this topic has been broached, as is evident from a report by Dagmar Reese and Carola Sachse on German research on women under national socialism (Reese and Sachse, 1990). In the 1970s feminist historians disproved the imputation that women voted predominantly for

Hitler by showing that in fact they tended to favour the conservatives. Feminists drew attention also to intellectual continuities between Nazi women and the women's movement of the Weimar Republic. They showed too that, contrary to popular perceptions, the national socialists did not have a coherent view of the nature and purpose of women; far from being a unified force, the party machine was riddled with conflicts and contradictions that gave opportunities to would-be dissidents. Feminists have also re-examined national socialism as a totally male-run system, and attempted to evaluate it in terms of patriarchy. Demands made on women (as child bearers, child rearers, housewives, party members, wage labourers and prostitutes) have been analysed in the light of feminist hopes for emancipation through paid employment, and attention drawn to the intermingling of the politics of race, population, the family and work. Considerable research has been done on women as resistance fighters. Because the national socialist emphasis on motherhood as reproduction reinforced a popular feminist belief that here lay the root of women's slavery, Gisela Bock's study of eugenic sterilisation campaigns came as a timely reminder of the anti-natalist thrust in national socialist policy, and that women were its prime victims (Bock, 1986). The forced sterilisation of Germans with genetic illnesses and the excesses of the Holocaust drew equally on eugenic notions of biologically 'inferior' life. Yet Bock has been accused of not differentiating sufficiently between selective sterilisation and mass murder. Other studies that show how adverse conditions in both the war and post-war periods enabled women to demonstrate their resilience and competence have been criticised for insensitivity to the horrors of the Nazi period. Finally, the trend to misuse or ignore historical facts in order to exonerate women reached its apogee in Margarete Mitscherlich's assertion that the psychic structure of women prevents them from being truly racist (Mitscherlich, 1983). As the women's movement did not prioritise the study of women's role under national socialism, research funding was always inadequate and such work received little encouragement or publicity. This partly explains the almost defamatory accusations levelled against women historians at the conference convened by Gravenhorst and Tatschmurat in 1990.

The difficulties experienced by the American historian Claudia Koonz in publishing a German translation of her 1987 book on *Mothers in the Fatherland*—which did not appear until 1991—were a further indication that the subject of women's complicity in Nazi society was not on the agenda. Koonz argues that, by retreating into their traditional role, women were able to live quite comfortably within this reputedly hostile regime. Moreover, the domestic sanctuary they provided enabled their men to endure the rigours of inhumanity. Such service did not go unrewarded. National socialism's policy of segregating the sexes resulted in the largest women's associations in history, which had a reasonable degree of autonomy as long as they did not interfere with the political agenda of the men. According to Koonz, there can be no doubt that women were active and interested participants in national socialism. While their exclusion from political power may have closed certain avenues of action, it opened up others. In 1990 the East German writer and psychologist, Helga Schubert, published a collection of interviews with women whose denunciations of others had resulted in the death of those denounced. Causing a considerable stir in Germany, *Judasfrauen* (Judas-Women) provided startling evidence that women were quite capable of self-determined evil action. It came out in the same year as another book on women collaborators by Martha Mamozai (1990).

In introducing the collection *Töchter-Fragen* ('daughter-questions') Gravenhorst (1990) calls on women to appropriate their past as a 'negative possession' (Jean Améry's term) and learn to live with it. Because Germany acted as a collective during the years of national socialism, only the victims of Nazi persecution can be exonerated. The subject of women's collaboration with national socialism needs to be debated by feminists openly and widely, and not merely (as hitherto) in the pages of obscure journals; furthermore, it needs to be approached from a moral rather than a cognitive or analytically descriptive point of view. Whether or not national socialism was patriarchal is irrelevant; what matters are the functions assumed by men and women within Nazi society. Gravenhorst warns that we must never forget that the actions of German men and women resulted in Auschwitz (Gravenhorst, 1990).

Although Gravenhorst's apparent indifference to the collection of accurate data about this complex period has aroused indignation among historians, her intervention has created the public debate she wanted, and women's motives for action have been scrutinised accordingly. Karin Windaus-Walser (Walser, 1990) draws attention to the fact that the cult of motherhood has always involved death as well as life. In proudly sending their sons off to war, the attitude of German mothers to the humans they had given birth to was every bit as instrumental and exploitative as that of which Adorno's and Horkheimer's *Dialectic of Enlightenment* accuses men. Claudia Bernardoni (1990) reinforces this connection when she reminds us that many women gloried in the cult of heroic bereavement, while Godele von der Decken's 1988 examination of women's literature produced during national socialism attests to a widespread understanding among women that motherhood is a position of superiority and dominance. In other words, women's fantasies appear to have been a powerful motivator of behaviour.

As Bernardoni (1990) points out, oppression often turns the oppressed into oppressors: it is the old story of the cabin-boy kicking the ship's cat. In Nazi Germany some women relished the power that the system gave them over those deemed racially or politically inferior, and used it to avenge themselves for perceived wrongs. Similarly, oppressed women and men alike took pride in the thought of being victors. For it must be kept in mind that, under fascism, men too were oppressed. The ethos of self-sacrifice imposed on them was associated traditionally with women, and the Nazis depended on a cult of masculinity to distract attention from the way they deprived men of masculine self-determination (d'Eramo, 1988:75). So it was not just a desire to be left in peace, as suggested by Thürmer-Rohr, that caused women to co-operate with the Nazis, nor was it simply the misguided hope of advancing further towards emancipation: clearly, emotional and subconscious factors also played a part. Finally, we need not assume that women reacted to national socialism primarily as women, for they were evidently attracted to its philosophies in much the same way as men were (Brockhaus, 1990). What research into national socialism has shown is that, even in a totally male-dominated society, women are not helpless, inactive or innocent. On the contrary, they make considered choices which are determined by individual circumstances, and consequently they have to take responsibility for their actions. Nothing in either their situation or their 'nature' can exonerate them from being accountable for what they do.

Taking action: tactical approaches to the liberation of women

We can now turn to Hippel's second recommendation, namely that women must fight their own battles. German women have twice had occasion to reflect on the wisdom of such advice. In 1918 they were granted the vote and full citizen's rights by the Social Democratic Party, although women themselves had not yet reached consensus on whether they wanted or deserved such rights. Fifteen years later those rights were largely lost with the advent of national socialism. Similarly, the progressive rights conferred on East German women by the state were lost almost completely with the unification of Germany in 1990. Because East German women had never had to fight for such rights, they had no experience in defending them, nor had they had opportunity to appreciate their full potential.

Before we begin to look at the activities of women, it is worth pausing to ask how women see themselves in relation to men. Should women be treated the same as men? Should women dissociate themselves from men? Or should men and women seek to reach a compromise with one another? This is not quite the same as asking whether women wish to perceive themselves as different from men, as essentially the same as men, or as androgynous. Nor does it distinguish the strategies of autonomy from those of equality. There is no consensus on these matters among German women. While feminists have developed autonomy to the point of separatism, career-minded women more often try to compete with men on masculinist terms, while those with a double or triple work-load usually prefer their men to take on some of the tasks and develop some of the qualities traditionally associated with women. There is no reason, of course, that the German women's movement should not benefit from a variety of approaches, but tolerance of difference has not always been conspicuous among German feminists.

German feminist activists have tended to assume that their particular project or cause would solve the problems of women in general. In an article on the 'forgotten difference', Gudrun-Axeli Knapp (1988) warns that the notion of women as a homogeneous group tends to rely on patriarchal stereotypes and will not help us to understand that the specific needs of women may vary widely, depending on such factors as class, race, ethnicity, upbringing, education, employment and personal situation. Where uniformity does in fact exist, it is likely to result from society's uniform expectations of women, which reduce them to their lowest common denominator. Knapp points out three errors that lead to abstract and unreal notions of 'woman': a methodological propensity for globalisation; an idealisation of 'woman' that ignores specific contexts; and a positivist attitude to what counts as reality. Generalisations, she warns, usually end up being prescriptive and consequently limiting and distorting. It is important to keep an open mind about the differences between women, and to define feminine subjectivity in a manner that allows for variety, heterogeneity, difference and idiosyncrasy.

Working outside the system

In choosing to call themselves autonomous (*autonome Frauen-bewegung),* radical German second-wave feminists indicate the extent to which autonomy has been a key concept for them. The philosophy of autonomy developed within a specific historical context and in the spirit of that Extra-Parliamentary-Opposition formed by students in the late 1960s, when a coalition of the major parties left Germany without an effective opposition—a situation that threw considerable doubt on the democratic intent of mainstream political practice. The diffuse structure of the second-wave women's movement can be seen, moreover, as a protest against those huge but largely unemancipated women's organisations that existed during both the Weimar Republic and the era of national socialism (Schenk, 1980:122ff.).

Lottemi Doormann (1979:65ff.) explains why women's groups of very different political persuasions agreed on the need for autonomy, if not for the same reasons. Women felt they needed spaces of their own in which to come to terms with themselves and develop their abilities without patriarchal surveillance. They also felt that the traditional exclusion of women and women's issues from all official parties and organisations warranted the founding of their own special-interest groups. Moreover, financial dependence on public funds administered by men would lead inevitably to patriarchal supervision and intervention, not to mention the delays caused by red tape. In its most radical form, female autonomy entailed separatist developments for women and the rejection of mainstream society.

The autonomous women's movement began with a campaign against abortion laws; when this was lost, a period of introversion and consciousness-raising ensued, followed by renewed activity (Lang, 1989:34ff.). Women's refuges, health and legal services, bookshops, restaurants, newsletters and magazines, publishing co-operatives, and self-help and discussion groups were founded. These enabled individual women to explore their needs and those of the women they met, and to experiment with solutions. Women attempted to construct a feminist public sphere that was not simply a marginalised alternative to mainstream society but rather an oppositional political force guided by feminist newsletters and magazines. Unfortunately, such publications are not always up to their task (Gruppe Feministische Öffentlichkeit, 1992). A recent version of this call for autonomy is Christina Thürmer-Rohr's *Vagabonding* (1991) which challenges women to commit themselves to 'homelessness' within existing society. Even women in politics have been reluctant to relinquish the notion of autonomy: an interview with four women politicians from the Green Party shows that they see in the marginality of their party opportunities for a dissident and subversive stance (Böttger et al., 1985).

But in the long term, the anarchist structures of the autonomous women's movement resulted in a lack of continuity and stability, and in a fragmentation and factionalisation that still characterises the German women's movement. Lack of money and a consequent dependence on volunteers means that projects tend to be limited in scope and hard to maintain. By rejecting mainstream politics, women have kept themselves out of positions of power and influence.

The autonomous women's movement began as a protest against the abortion law. Such protests and demonstrations have always been at the centre of its political activity, and more recently it has experimented with the kind of industrial action normally taken by workers who consider themselves to be exploited. Traditionally, women have been exploited in both their housework and their contribution to society (and ultimately industry) as child-bearers. It is therefore not surprising that women should have exercised strike action in these two areas. For some years, a small but vocal group of women has conducted a reproductive strike (*Gebärstreik*). In the wake of unification (prior to which East German women had better access than West Germans to abortion) and after the Constitutional Court's negative decision on liberal amendments to the abortion law in 1993, a one-day general strike by women was planned. It aimed to publicise the depth of female discontent and to make visible female solidarity, while drawing attention to the extensive disruptions that would be caused if women were to withhold their unpaid services. However, it had neither the support nor the impact hoped for by the organisers.

Some perceptions of autonomy, however, are decidedly non-political and separatist. The *affidamento* movement (discussed in Chapter 4, pp. 66–7) calls on women to develop a culture of their own in accordance with their quite separate nature, values and purpose in life. It therefore eschews all attempts to influence the patriarchal public sphere by aiming for equality within it. Alternative life-styles—from witches' covens to rural communes—have also attracted German women. Similarly, lesbian women have begun to develop a culture of their own. Sabine Hark (1989) has drawn attention to lesbian communities as constituting the first observable non-patriarchal social group, and noted the amazing diversity of life-styles developed by these women, especially in California. Such models enable women to appreciate the variety of choices available to them once they are no longer under pressure to conform to the social structures in which heterosexual women have lived for millennia.

Recently, the philosophy of 'separate spheres'—so prominent during the first wave of the women's movement—has been revived. In response to Chernobyl, a group of German women supported by the Green Party issued a *Müttermanifest* ('mothers' manifesto') calling for a re-evaluation of motherhood as a woman's true calling. Mothers who want to be housewives should receive support, whereas working mothers should be given child-care facilities and shorter working hours in recognition of their reproductive contribution to society. This initiative draws on the ideas of Gisela Erler (1978), who believes that the professionalisation of caring services (which the women's movement indirectly promotes in demanding that all women's work be accredited financially) hinders the development of neighbourhood networks based on friendship and trust. Paid social work tends to be characterised by impersonality, impermanence, professional duty and a hierarchical relationship between worker and client. From the point of view of non-working mothers (who were still the majority in the former FRG, as they are in reunited Germany today), community work allows an escape from the narrow confines of the home and provides opportunities for rewarding experiences. If such avenues of activity are blocked, the lives of most German women will become even more depleted. As non-working mothers have more time to consider the changes to women's lives that need to be made and to build up networks and support structures, they can make important contributions to the women's movement. Although fully aware of the argument that women should not give society even more for nothing, Erler suggests that to strengthen the position of non-working mothers with unspecified payments is a better way to go. A humane society, she maintains, cannot exist if people are prevented from doing voluntary work for the love of others. Far from wanting all women back in the home, Erler argues for a two-track approach to women's liberation. She reiterated and popularised her ideas in *Frauenzimmer* (1985), a book that made an impact on Green Party policy in the mid-1980s. But it met with protest from feminists such as Haug (1988) and Böttger (1987), who see as retrograde both her exoneration of fathers from parental responsibilities and the implied devaluation of employment and education for women.

Working within the system

In German the word *Gleichheit* means both 'sameness' and 'equality'. This has made it more difficult, perhaps, for German women to work out what it is that they really want. Cornelia Edding seems to subscribe to an ideal of sameness in her *Einbruch in den Herrenclub* (1983), a collection of interviews with women in high-powered positions which registers mainly disappointment. In their research report on the subject of women and work, Angelika Wetterer and Brigitte Robak (1992) stress the importance of differentiating carefully between men and women, as well as between women of different historical periods, social classes, and marital and family status, all of whom often have quite different needs. Nevertheless, many working women are likely to agree with the statement—used in the title of a book of interviews with working-class women obliged to alternate between family and factory—that 'one [job] is too little—two are too much' (Becker-Schmidt et al., 1984, my trans.). There are no easy solutions to this dilemma, though there is plenty of advice. It seems particularly important to make sure of three things: that equal rights guaranteed by the constitution are reinforced by legislation; that society provides support to working mothers; and that men do their share of domestic and family duties. Elisabeth Beck-Gernsheim (1984) argues that neither demographers nor child psychologists have been able to produce valid reasons for discouraging mothers from taking paid employment. Whether or not the introduction of employment quotas would benefit women is hotly debated (Lang, 1989).

It has taken the German women's movement almost two decades to take to heart what Hannelore Mabry had said in 1971, that women will not get far without representation in parliament and on official bodies (Mabry, 1974). Various attempts to form a women's party, also one of Mabry's suggestions (1974), have failed. At present the Green Party has both the most favourable structure and the most emancipatory policies for women, although it has had conservative and male-chauvinist elements. In short-lived Red–Green coalitions in both the state of Hessen (1985) and the senate of Berlin (1989) women from the Green Party played a dominant role. Later, during the most recent phase (1992–93) of the struggle for abortion rights, women set an important precedent for solidarity by forming a pro-abortion alliance across all parties. In 1994 a feminist lawyer, Jutta Limbach, was appointed president of the Constitutional Court, an institution deemed by pro-abortionists to be particularly reactionary in matters related to women, since it has twice blocked liberal amendments to the abortion law.

Parliamentary activity requires a considerable adjustment to patriarchal structures, but Green women parliamentarians have certainly attempted to change traditional political attitudes and practices. In her study of German women politicians in the Berlin Senate during 1989 and 1990, Barbara Schaeffer-Hegel (1992) has been able to show how these women aimed (against great odds) at achieving a new and more humane political culture. This involved lateral thinking, the maintenance of a wider (and not merely job-related) network, a more relaxed attitude to time, a recognition of issues beyond their own portfolios that required serious consideration, even if this entailed a loss of resources for their own work, and experimenting with more democratic types of advisory bodies. Though most of the women studied by Schaeffer-Hegel did not survive the politically fraught process of unification, the work they did indicates that women in the public sphere may eventually effect changes to patriarchal society.

One important strategy for integrating women into society has been to increase their visibility. Green women parliamentarians saw this as a central concern. To some extent, the enormously increased involvement by women in literature, film, art and the media has served that purpose. So too has West German feminist linguistic reform. In contrast to both East German usage (where women professionals were designated by the generic masculine form) and English 'gender-neutral' language, West German women have insisted on using—or including by means of a slash—the feminine endings or pronouns in all cases where a woman is or might be involved. As a result, cumbersome and often barely manageable—but consequently all the more noticeable—structures are now inescapably part of all official documents. It is felt that the integration of women into society can be successful only if constant attention is given to their presence and their needs (Trömel-Plötz, 1982, 1984; Pusch, 1984).

It would appear that autonomy and equality are virtually incompatible goals. This has led to a great deal of factionalism and infighting within the German women's movement. In an article inspired by a post-Chernobyl conference where such disagreements had been particularly painful, Barbara Böttger (1987) pleads that what is needed is not conflict but a two-track approach. Women can never be either completely equal with men or completely different from them. While socialisation has produced in women strengths they should not forfeit, they will not achieve anything unless they participate in mainstream culture and share power. Differences of opinion should be fruitful rather than divisive. Polls show that most German women want to have children as well as an education and a profession. Here is proof that the women's movement needs to facilitate both desires.

Working towards a revolution

In the early years of the second wave of the women's movement, feminists tended to position themselves and their concerns within the wider context of revolutionary socialism. But disillusionment set in very quickly; like Marx and Engels before them, the men who ran the socialist student groups categorised the emancipation of women as a matter of secondary importance. Frigga Haug had been a socialist of some years standing when she joined the women's movement in 1968, and never relinquished her loyalties to socialism. Challenged to justify her split allegiance, Haug (1981) admits that the economic oppression of the proletariat by capitalism is unrelated to the oppression of women in patriarchal society, and that attempts to link them directly have been driven generally by dogmatism. Nevertheless, she says, the implications and effects of certain constantly shifting and indirect links need to be examined. Any politics that ignores the complex relationships between these two power systems is unlikely to resist either of them effectively. For example, certain structural changes in the printing industry made male typesetters redundant and thereby favoured female workers, who received lower pay because traditionally they are considered to be less skilled. Unions opposed those changes so vigorously in favour of men that they lost the opportunity to upgrade the work and pay of women, and consequently the employer ended up as the beneficiary. In this case the unions confused industrial with patriarchal politics to the detriment of both oppressed groups. Whereas women cannot afford to ignore industrial politics, unions must make it their business to be aware of women's struggle for equality. As far as Haug is concerned, socialism and feminism are equally revolutionary programmes for achieving an egalitarian society.

Although the women who work as social analysts with Maria Mies rely considerably on socialist economic theory, they advocate a different and more fundamental kind of change. Mies relates the dehumanising tendencies of modern capitalist and socialist economies to the 'dichotomy between life-producing and preserving and commodity-producing activities' (Mies and Shiva, 1993:321). Like the British economist Malcolm Caldwell, she believes that by returning to a subsistence perspective we can solve the problems not only of modern society but also of women in Third World countries, who typically are trapped in a subsistence sector that is undermined and downgraded by the modern market economy. A subsistence economy, by contrast, emphasises use-value: 'self-provisioning, self-sufficiency, particularly in food and other basic needs; regionality; and decentralisation from a state bureaucracy are the main economic principles. The local and regional resources are used but not exploited; the market plays a subordinate role' (ibid.:319). In such an economy, relationships with both nature and other people would change. Grass-roots democracy would be promoted and problem-solving would become multi-dimensional. Technology would be guided by an 'ecologically sound, feminist, subsistence science' (ibid.:320). A 'reintegration of culture and work' (ibid.) would lead to a more holistic approach to life. Such a society would be feminist because Mies's vision is modelled not on the male wage-earner (as in Marxist theory) but on the mother and housewife. Mies describes individual projects undertaken in Third World countries and by alternative groups in the west. But as Barbara Böttger (1987) points out, even if a subsistence economy were able to solve all human problems, it is difficult to envisage how it might be implemented or enforced on a major scale when the global economy is moving in the opposite direction. Nevertheless, communities in countries where capitalism is not yet firmly entrenched might benefit from returning to a communal and subsistence-based life-style that makes them independent of cash crops and the World Bank. Problematically, Mies's approach prescribes one solution for everyone, without taking account of historical, geographical and cultural differences. It also assumes not only that the clock can simply be turned back, but also that people—and particularly women—were better off in premodern societies. Because its perspective is predominantly economic, it ignores the point made by the physicist and political scientist Elvira Scheich (1987) that the problems created by advanced science can be solved only by still more advanced science. The radioactive materials processed this century will be a problem for humanity for the next 24 000 years. Similarly, gene technology can radically alter all forms of life. Such developments have changed the relationship between politics and science, in so far as politics is no longer in control. Those who turn their backs on scientific progress forfeit their opportunity to influence the course of events.

A more light-hearted approach to feminist revolutionary thinking is the anarchic pluralism advocated by the Austrian feminist Erica Fischer (1989), whose article on 'mounting accidents' exuberates in radical and mischievous resistance. A feminist revolution manifests itself in her view as

a creeping destabilisation, subversion lying in wait, perceived by the male public as a slight irritation, a barely perceptible realignment of the accustomed reactions of women, a change of paradigm that is annoying like an itch but very soon can no longer be localised. Interspersed with shock-like raids on male perceptions of themselves. (ibid.:72, my trans.)

Her catalogue of symptoms becomes more specific:

broken film projectors, viruses in computer programs, children in the council chambers, unmade beds, peculiarly slow looms. Strikes by women students to exclude men from the study of gynaecology, listing the names of rapists and violent husbands in department stores, businesses and train stations, a female photographer in front of every pornographic shop, sudden changes of direction where they are least expected, sales-women who refuse to smile at men, waitresses who show women to the best table, secretaries who give precedence to female job applicants, television announcers who retrieve women's sporting news from wastepaper baskets, female MPs who mention things in Parliament that make their male colleagues lose their cool. (ibid.:73, my trans.).

Women, she claims, have it easy: they can recognise each other, they are not locked away in ghettos, they are familiar with the world of men, and they can move around in it at high speed. They are indispensable to men both as labourers and lovers, and they are willing to co-operate with men who behave themselves. The complex ties between men and women make it difficult for the state to intervene. And since women travel and talk to other women, every initiative taken in one country is likely to be repeated in another. Differences between women lead to pro-ductive debate. It is up to women to act in a hundred different ways, each one appropriate to the occasion. For while women unquestionably deserve a better deal, the world, Fischer reminds us, desperately needs radical change.

8

Women and Knowledge

Academic, scientific and technological professions have traditionally been virtual men's clubs. In a collection entitled *Wie männlich ist die Wissenschaft?*, sixteen women from a wide variety of disciplines comment on the reasons for this fact (Hausen and Nowotny, 1986).

In our own and almost every other culture, language, philosophy, scholarship and science are masculine institutions. What does this imply for women? Should women develop a new feminine model of knowledge? Is a critique of existing theory the way to go? Do women need a different intellectual and scientific practice, or a new research ethos? Or is it enough to simply fill in the blank spots in existing systems of knowledge?

A new model: feminist knowledge as Utopia

Eva Meyer (1983, 1984) is one of the few German feminist thinkers to envisage a new model, based on French post-structural theory. Her point of departure is a situation commonly encountered by women: that their 'understanding' is often not meaningful to them. For 'the feminine is no language' (Meyer, 1984b:47, my trans.); women can express themselves as women only on the margins of conceptual language, through images or, more precisely, images of woman. Admittedly, a discourse could be developed from that position, but do women really want a feminist hermeneutics (ibid.:48)? Should they not rather attempt to dissolve the forms of logical organisation and rethink them? Meyer points out that women have more than images at their disposal. Women also have access to what she terms 'the order of the legend, which makes of a hypothesised whole pieces that can be read and which serve to reveal a strategic organisation' (ibid.), and there are non-representational signs like letters and numbers which resist interpretation. Instead of thinking of meaning as a fortress to be stormed, we can imagine it as a labyrinth which requires us to be short-sighted and in transit. This is the way to read a legend. From Plato onwards, we have had an anthropo-morphic view of language that implies a unified consciousness. Misfits are disposed of as legend 'with its demons and changelings' and 'significant leftovers, that inscribe themselves into the interstices and turn definition into movement' (ibid.:50). 'Legend' is aligned with 'woman' and pursued through the labyrinth, which is 'equally open and closed . . . [and] shows the connecting and the non-connecting paths, where being on the move is both a journey and no progress' (ibid.). Women must invent this labyrinth, 'which confuses him who still believes that the world can in principle be understood and represented' (ibid.:52) for there 'the self-description of the woman is set in motion' (ibid.:51, my translations). This volume takes its intentionally ambiguous title from the first essay 'Versprechen'. On one hand, it refers to the wilful 'mis-speaking' that Meyer recommends and practises against what she sees as the repressive regime of normative language and logical meaning. But it also evokes the 'promise' of new possibilities of perception and understanding opened up, in her view, by a deconstructive style of writing designed to dismantle the ideology of 'universal man'.

A critical practice: feminist knowledge as dissidence

Meyer's utopian model of feminist knowledge is less representative in the German-speaking region than the counter-model of feminist knowledge as critical practice. Whereas Meyer seeks to open up a space for thought *beyond* patriarchal knowledge, other German feminists such as Marianne Schuller prefer to occupy a position of 'dissidence' within existing systems of knowledge. In two articles first published in 1979, Schuller represents the feminine as both the shadow against which the imaginary scenarios of male literary production are played out (1990b) and as the nightside of the human sciences (1979). She exposes the exclusionary mechanisms for constructing knowledge in the humanities, and especially in traditional literary studies. Most notable is the orthodoxy of literature as reconciliation (Freier, 1976), which supposes that in literature the hostile forces of life achieve harmonious balance. This is reinforced in fiction by the practice of inviting readers to identify with literary characters, worlds and philosophies. In such practices, Schuller argues, thought is commonly figured as acquisition rather than encounter, and the corresponding idea of order is based on separation and negation—especially separation from and negation of women (Schuller, 1990b). In analysing Hegel, Schuller (1979) shows how the category of universal man (as the subject of knowledge in the humanities) presupposes not only the negation of difference but also the suppression of memories of origins in the dark 'nether regions' of the feminine sphere. Because such memories remain an internal enemy in privileged texts of the human sciences, Schuller suggests that the role of feminist textual criticism is to raise them to consciousness. This project is comparable to Brigitte Weißhaupt's proposals for a sensitisation of reason. But whereas Schuller's primary concern is to subvert the symbolic order of masculine knowledge, Weißhaupt (1986a) insists that the feminist critique of reason (in the reductive sense of instrumental rationality) cannot afford to dispense with reason altogether. She thus defines the feminist critique of prevailing ideologies of enlightenment as a practice of dissidence, that is, the disclosure that things are other than they have been believed to be.

Another major form of dissident German feminist theory is the critique of the logic and research practices of modern science. Elisabeth List (1990) has drawn attention to A. N. Whitehead's observation that because modern science was scripted by ancient Greek tragedians, we have been led to believe ourselves subject to a tragic and inexorable fate, against which it is pointless to intervene. Drawing on and extending Adorno's and Horkheimer's critique, Ursula Beer (1987a) investigates the theological origins of the belief that men hold dominion over both women and nature, and the connection between this belief and an irrational hope for immortality. According to Christine Woesler (1987), the kind of abstraction practised by modern science was introduced in the custom of barter, which abstracts goods from their real-life use, and operates with such concepts as exclusive ownership and indifference to the labour incorporated in bartered goods. Woesler points out that these forms of abstraction are central to both modern science and the exchange of goods, where use, usefulness and concreteness are relatively insignificant. The structural shift from the real abstractions of barter to the mental abstractions of science has resulted in significant blind spots to (among other things) the nature and social contributions of women. The sciences of midwifery and healing—once practised by women—stood in a direct relationship to nature. But because the cognitive patterns of science are essentially extraneous to nature, they are more likely to lead to unrealistic thinking.

Because the nature and structure of science have been determined largely by men, it embodies their gender characteristics. Elisabeth List (1990) quotes Evelyn Fox Keller's theory that because men need to detach themselves from their pre-Oedipal mothers they are obsessed with objectivity, and that this has left its mark on all the sciences. Rosemarie Rübsamen (1983) sees the sciences as driven by the same aggressive and hierarchical male competitiveness that dominates the political scene. The emphasis of science on war and high-tech equipment bears this out. Whatever predisposes men to this competitive behaviour—their hormones, a need to compensate for women's procreative ability, or the misogynistic exclusion of women from power—results in a way of life that is alien to women. Not surprisingly, science itself has been affected by the competitive behaviour of scientists. Thus the natural sciences are organised hierarchically, with the inorganic sciences of mathematics and physics dominating the biological sciences. In physics, the smallest and most abstract particle—the rishon (in Hebrew 'the first', in Arabic 'the boss')—is perceived to head the pyramid. Rübsamen explains that there is nothing 'natural' or inevitable about the present structure of the natural sciences.

Western science, in reducing living things to assemblages of inorganic particles, does little to help us understand the secrets of life. The view that science is driven by humankind's natural curiosity is a myth. A science which privileges the inorganic can then tamper with complex natural structures in order to dominate and exploit nature. The fact that these hierarchical structures result in inefficiencies is for Rübsamen further evidence of science's desire to control and dominate. To be effective, such structures demand an interdisciplinary approach which, given the complexity of modern science, cannot be implemented: no biologist can be both a chemist and a physicist in ways that significantly further his or her research. As an essentially masculinist project, science is for Rübsamen fundamentally flawed. But paradoxically, modern science and technology, as Elvira Scheich (1987) points out, have created a situation in which more science is now required to help us deal with the problems that they have generated. This view is reiterated in her recent book *Naturbeherrschung und Weiblichkeit* ('domination of nature and femininity') (1993), an investigation of the connections between the scientific approach to nature and socially constructed gender differences. She argues for a mode of feminist critique which, taking full account of the dialectic of enlightenment, is itself dialectical (ibid.:7–9). Scheich, herself a physicist as well as a political scientist, opposes the call for a completely different concept of nature. The androcentric distortions of scientific thinking (and the ecological depredations of its practical application) can be countered, not by simply reversing the binary dualisms on which it is based, but only by critical reflection upon its social unconscious.

The feminist critique of research methodology: partiality, interdisciplinarity, commitment

One reason feminist social theory can never be radically new is that, because theories exist within a current social system, they must be relevant to it if they are to be useful. Given the multiplicity of social theories available today, the task of feminist researchers is to select, criticise, modify and adapt them to women's needs, insights and perspectives; in other words, to subject them to what Marlis Krüger (1987:80) calls hermetic exploitation, putting them to a use other than that originally intended. Two particularly useful types of theory have been critical social research and emancipatory social research. In this respect, German feminists benefited from aligning themselves with Critical Theory in the so-called *Positivismus-Streit* of 1972, a controversy between the positivist Karl Popper and social theorist Theodor Adorno. What Popper defended above all was the principle of objectivity. But as Ursula Beer (1987c) shows, Adorno never suggested that objectivity could be dispensed with. He simply defined it differently by providing an alternative conception of truth, based on the theory of knowledge developed by Ludwig Feuerbach and Karl Marx. In the dialectic epistemology of Adorno's Critical Theory, objective knowledge has three main characteristics: it serves a rational society that is free from exploitation and oppression; it requires commitment and therewith partiality, which implies a feminist emphasis on experience and emotionality; and it is measured by the degree to which it relates to society as a whole. Objective statements are often contradictory because almost inevitably so are social relations: contradictoriness should not be equated with irrationality, as it is by positivists. While giving credit where it is due, Beer points out that the totality envisaged in Critical Theory is diminished, unfortunately, by gender blindness and its practice, therefore, could be improved upon. Ulrike Büchner (1984) draws attention to the inherent paternalism of Critical Theory; for instead of drawing those who constitute the 'object' of research into the research process, it limits itself to confronting them with results and recommendations which they are expected to act upon. Emancipatory research, by contrast, gives the objects of research an active role in the research process.

Feminist research practice

The first German feminist to advocate emancipatory research was Maria Mies (1978). Her work in India heightened her awareness that most social science projects serve to stabilise existing structures of dominance, because ordinary people often volunteer inaccurate answers, if they feel that this will please researchers whom they think of as superiors. Since female researchers are considered socially inferior, however, they often have a better chance of obtaining honest responses. Mies drew attention to the fact that none of the new developments coming out of the positivism debate in Critical Theory, Marxism and action research had managed to get beyond that stringent separation of theory from practice advocated by conventional social science. As the philosopher and educationalist Paulo Freire (1993) had observed, the culture of silence characteristic of oppressed people—and women belong to this category—can be overcome only by means of fundamental changes to their lives.

In this context, Mies points out that as social scientists women tend to be both subjects and objects of their research. But instead of deploring this, women should examine the possibilities opened up to them by such a double consciousness. For while it makes them more sensitive than men to the psychological mechanisms of dominance, self-interest compels them to be alert to the motives and mechanisms of suppression. Consequently, women are well placed to critique social science.

Mies goes on to specify seven postulates for feminist social research: conscious involvement of the researcher in the project; working in the service of the oppressed; active participation in emancipatory struggles by integrating research into them; perceiving that to study something you have to change it (but for the changes brought about by the women's movement, there would be no feminist research); choosing an area of research that supports current struggles; handing on the results and techniques of research to those who are the objects of it so that they can use and benefit from it; and realising that feminist social theory must emerge from participation in the struggles of the women's movement. To illustrate how feminist action and feminist research can mesh productively with one another, Mies describes how both academics and non-academics co-operated in a project (in which she herself was involved) to build a women's shelter in Cologne.

Mies's essay created a new feminist consciousness about the theory and methodology of research. Its strongly egalitarian, emancipatory and activist impulses were taken up and often refined by others, who expect researchers to become more self-critical and more daringly interdisciplinary.

In this context, the 'memory work' of Frigga Haug and Kornelia Hauser (1985–86) deserves to be examined closely (Haug, 1992). Both were dissatisfied with the practices of consciousness-raising groups which merely allowed women to let off steam and then return pacified to an unaltered home situation. Because the women's problems were usually not analysed or theorised—or even recorded—such groups were therapeutically, politically and scientifically ineffective. Haug and Hauser set out to remedy this.

They invited women to attend group sessions on a single theme, such as 'responsibility' or 'the body'. Relevant theoretical texts were studied and discussed before the women were asked to write down as faithfully as possible their memories of any incident relating to such a topic. These accounts were then examined by the whole group—not only for what they said, but also for what they did not say, or said inadequately or unconvincingly. This probing critique was made possible, therefore, by a combination of theoretical knowledge and personal experiences (and courage). While allowing all the women to speak about their problems in a focused and constructive way, it forced the writer of the day to retrieve her suppressed memories, revise her accustomed perception of events, and face up to her own evasiveness and forgetfulness. Once the topics had been discussed conclusively, the results were written up and published.

Haug and Hauser's methodology requires both committed researchers and active and developing subject/objects of research, all working together to achieve individual and social change. It is interdisciplinary in so far as it incorporates social theory, techniques of literary criticism, and psycho-therapeutical methods of group interaction and discussion. By amending the practices of consciousness-raising groups, it aims to help women overcome the psychological damage inflicted by their socialisation. Unlike Freudian therapy, which persuades people to accept their lot, this therapy enables them to change it. The psychologist whose theories Haug and Hauser draw upon is K. Holzkamp: he founded Critical Psychology, a school of psychology indebted to Adorno's Critical Theory, in which the central concept is enablement.

The ethnopsychoanalyst Maja Nadig (1985, 1986) attempts to

fuse three different disciplines: critical ethnology, a socially focused psychoanalysis, and feminist sociology. Critical ethnology is useful, she explains, in emphasising the point of view of the oppressed on the relationship between the hegemonic and the marginal. Oppression of this kind can be found in unfamiliar cultures, fringe groups, and low castes and classes. By means of 'empathetic observation', critical ethnology effectively counters colonialist attitudes but not those defence mechanisms which enable a researcher to exoticise, idealise or devalue the unfamiliar. By turning to another discipline, psychoanalysis, researchers can come to terms with unconscious reactions in both themselves and their respondents, and understand the dialectic relationship in which transferences take place. However, Nadig admits that one disadvantage of the psychoanalytic approach is that it requires researchers to use a method that is not only inflexible but of dubious value to feminists on account of the notorious phallocentrism of psychoanalytic theory (Becker-Schmidt, 1985).

In practice, Nadig's method entails complementing reports on her observations with a day-by-day diary of personal responses and reactions, which the researcher can analyse with the help of a counsellor. Such a diary helped Nadig to recognise her panic reactions to the flood of information that overwhelmed her when she first arrived in Mexico to study Daxho Indian women and which led to premature categorisations and explanations, ill-considered paternalistic behaviour when approached for money, initial unease with local attitudes to space and time, and varying Daxho suspicions of her as rich white woman, communist, spy and missionary. She formed complex relationships with individual women, who were often slow to recognise and admit their real concerns and analyse them productively. The aim was not only to study how women in that traditional society tackled their problems, but to conduct the research in such a way that they themselves would acquire an understanding and skills that would help them. In a later study, Nadig (1992) showed how the same methodology could be employed to understand and support Swiss village women.

While an awareness of the differing subjectivities of both researcher and researched has led to interesting results in these three cases, there are limits to its usefulness. As Marlis Krüger (1987) observes, it is perfectly normal for people to alternate between subject and object status. Regina Becker-Schmidt (1985) warns of methodological problems associated with subject status. The female researcher who is both involved as a woman and detached as an investigator needs to be fully aware of her dual role. Her involvement encourages both empathy and an introspection, which, although it will further her understanding of the people and problems she is studying, will unfortunately not increase her ability to understand differences. Even empathetic understanding can not be relied upon, partly because the researcher may be led astray by her different experiences, and partly because both researcher and researched may well have the same blind spots. Moreover, since the subject of feminist research ('woman') is as yet undefined, any attempt to provide a positive definition is problematic. Becker-Schmidt warns that potential traps include seeing women as merely passive victims; gender-reversing the masculine hierarchy of values in order to place women 'ahead'; claiming for women everything not yet designated masculine; and postulating an essential and uniform femininity.

Some German feminists have recently questioned not only the overvaluation of subjectivity, empathy and partiality but also an earlier feminist insistence that social theory should be tied to political praxis. A preoccupation with the practical and political implications of theoretical concepts (which has been particularly prevalent in German feminism) has sometimes acted as a block to innovative thinking, as Hagemann-White argues in the introduction to a volume on women's images of men and masculinity, *FrauenMännerBilder* (Hagemann-White and Rerrich, 1988:9). Within the humanities, some German feminist theorists have also taken up the post-structuralist argument that writing is in itself a form of praxis, and as such can be just as subversive as (and in the long term possibly more radically transformative than) the changes brought about by the kind of old-style political activism, valorised, for example, by Mies. This is what Meyer seems to believe. In the German context, it is not difficult to understand the persistence of socially critical, historically oriented and politically committed modes of feminist research, or indeed the resistance to what is widely seen as an ahistorical and irresponsible form of intellectual free play. This heightened sense of social responsibility is in part a response to reckoning with the Nazi past, especially the widespread failure of German academics and intellectuals to resist Hitler's rise to power. Even when that history is not made explicit, in our view it has contributed to the ferocity of recent debates in Germany between activist and textualist feminists. However, as the editors of a collection of essays on precisely this issue indicate, these different approaches need not be mutually exclusive (Brügmann and Kublitz-Kramer, 1993). German advocates of a politically engaged mode of feminist knowledge frequently pit Critical Theory against post-structuralism. But as Sigrid Weigel observes in the introduction to another recent volume which seeks to move beyond this kind of polarisation of positions, many productive correspondences can be established between the work of the early Frankfurt School and contemporary French theory (Weigel, 1995:5) On the question of feminist intellectual strategies, Gisela Ecker (1988), whose own work exemplifies such an alliance, has argued convincingly that women should act on many levels and maintain an angry praxis of political resistance while simultaneously developing a utopian praxis of playful deconstructive reading and writing.

In both its practical and theoretical dimensions, German feminism has been characterised at times by factions, fissures and an intolerance of difference. Today, however, there seems to be a greater recognition of the inevitability and indeed desirability of a plurality of approaches reflecting the heterogeneity of women and the complexity of feminist transformation. Moreover, the endeavour of some theorists to break through the stalemate between conflicting positions is opening up new horizons for feminist thinking. Post-structuralist approaches have clearly had a powerful impact on German feminist theory over the past decade, especially in the area of literary and cultural studies (see, for example, Lindhoff, 1995). However, the continuing importance of other traditions of cultural critique and philosophical reflection and the significance of the historical memories that shape the context of intellectual discussions in Germany guarantee that German-speaking women will continue to make a distinctive contribution to feminist thinking in the years to come—a contribution that will, we hope, also gain the recognition that it deserves outside the German-speaking region in future.

Bibliography

Adorno, T. and M. Horkheimer (1989) *Dialectic of Enlightenment*, trans. J. Cumming, London and New York: Verso [Ger 1944]

Akashe-Böhme, F. (1991) 'Selbstbestimmung an der Grenze der Natur' in Konnertz (ed.) *Grenzen der Moral*, pp. 13–29

Althoff, G. (1991) *Weiblichkeit als Kunst. Die Geschichte eines kulturellen Deutungsmusters*, Stuttgart: Metzler

Altner, G. (ed.) (1987) *Ökologische Theologie—Perspektiven zur Orientierung*, Stuttgart: Kreuz

Amendt, G. (1992) *Das Leben unerwünschter Kinder*, Frankfurt am Main: Fischer

Andreas-Grisebach, M. and B. Weißhaupt (eds) (1986) *Was Philosophinnen denken*, vol. 2, Zurich: Ammann

Andresen, H. (1988) 'Weibliches Sprechen—weibliches Denken—weibliches Gehirn? Zur These geschlechtsspezifischer Unterschiede menschlicher Gehirne' in U. Aumüller-Roske (ed.) *Frauenleben—Frauenbilder—Frauengeschichte*, Pfaffenweiler: Centaurus, pp. 1–16

Appich, M. et al. (eds) (1993) *Eine andere Tradition. Dissidente Positionen von Frauen in Philosophie und Theologie*, Munich: Iudicum

Bachmann, I. (1990) *Malina. A Novel*, trans. P. Boehm, New York: Holmes and Meier [Ger 1977]

Bachofen, J. J. (1948) *Das Mutterrecht. Eine Untersuchung über die Gynaekokratie der alten Welt nach ihrer religiösen und rechtlichen Natur* [1861] in *Gesammelte Werke*, vols 2 and 3, ed. K. Meuli, Basel: Benno Schwabe

—— (1967) *Myth, Religion, and Mother Right: Selected Writings of J. J. Bachofen*, trans. R. Mannheim, intros G. Boas and J. Campbell, London: Routledge and Kegan Paul, pp. 69–207

Barta, I. (1984) 'Maria Theresia—Kritik einer Rezeption' in Bechtel et al. (eds) (1984) *Die ungeschriebene Geschichte*, pp. 337–57

Barta, I. et al. (eds) (1987) *Frauen Bilder Männer Mythen. Kunsthistorische Beiträge*, Berlin: Reimer

Baudrillard, J. (1994) *Simulacra and Simulation*, trans. S. F. Glaser, Ann Arbor: University of Michigan Press [Fr 1981]

Beauvoir, S. de (1953) *The Second Sex*, trans. H. M. Parshley, New York: Alfred A. Knopf [Fr 1949]

Bechtel, B. et al. (eds) (1984) *Die ungeschriebene Geschichte. Historische Frauenforschung. Dokumentation des 5. Historikerinnentreffens in Wien*, Vienna: Wiener Frauenverlag

Beck-Gernsheim, E. (1984) *Vom Geburtenrückgang zur Neuen Mütterlichkeit? Über private und politische Interessen am Kind*, Frankfurt am Main: Fischer

Beck-Gernsheim, E. and U. Beck (1989) *Das ganz normale Chaos der Liebe*, Frankfurt am Main: Suhrkamp

Becker, R. (1992) *Inszenierungen des Weiblichen. Die literarische Darstellung weiblicher Subjektivität in der westdeutschen Frauenliteratur der siebziger und achtziger Jahre*, Frankfurt am Main: Lang

Becker-Schmidt, R. (1985) 'Probleme einer feministischen Theorie und Empirie in den Sozialwissenschaften', *Feministische Studien* 3, 2, pp. 93–104

—— (1987) 'Frauen und Deklassierung. Geschlecht und Klasse' in Beer (ed.) (1987a), pp. 213–66

—— (1989) 'Identitätslogik und Gewalt. Zum Verhältnis von Kritischer Theorie und Feminismus', *Beiträge zur feministischen Theorie und Praxis* 12, 24, pp. 51–64

Becker-Schmidt, R. et al. (1984) *Eines ist zuwenig—Beides ist zuviel. Erfahrungen von Arbeiterfrauen zwischen Familie und Fabrik*, Bonn: Neue Gesellschaft

Beer, U. (ed.) (1987a) *Klasse Geschlecht. Feministische Gesellschaftsanalyse und Wissenschaftskritik*, Bielefeld: AJZ

—— (1987b) 'Herrschaft über Natur und Menschen als Gegenstand feministischer Gesellschaftsanalyse und Wissenschaftskritik' in Beer (ed.) *Klasse Geschlecht*, pp. 1–27

—— (1987c) 'Objektivität und Parteilichkeit—Ein Widerspruch in feministischer Forschung? Zur Erkenntnisproblematik von Geschlechtsstruktur' in Beer (ed.) *Klasse Geschlecht*, pp. 162–212

—— (1988) 'Das Zwangsjackett des bürgerlichen Selbst—Instrumentelle Vernunft und Triebverzicht' in Kulke (ed.) *Rationalität und sinnliche Vernunft*, pp. 16–29

Bendkowsky, H. and B. Weißhaupt (eds) (1983) *Was Philosophinnen denken. Eine Dokumentation*, Zurich: Ammann

Benjamin, W. (1973) *Illuminations*, ed. and intro. H. Arendt, trans. H. Zohn, London: Fontana [Ger 1955]

Bennholdt-Thomsen, V. (1987) 'Die Ökologiefrage ist eine Frauenfrage' in Die GRÜNEN im Bundestag (eds) *Frauen und Ökologie*, pp. 29–38

Berger, R. et al. (eds) (1985) *Frauen, Weiblichkeit, Schrift. Dokumentation der Tagung in Bielefeld, Juni 1984*, Berlin: Argument

Berger, R. and I. Stephan (eds) (1987) *Weiblichkeit und Tod in der Literatur*, Cologne and Vienna: Böhlau

Bernard, C. and E. Schlaffer (1984) *Sozialwissenschaft und politische Bildung*, Vienna: Verlag für Geschichte und Politik

Bernardoni, C. (1990) 'Ohne Schuld und Sühne? Der moralische Diskurs über die feministische Auseinandersetzung mit dem Nationalsozialismus' in Gravenhorst and Tatschmurat (eds) *Töchter-Fragen*, pp. 127–34

Bettelheim, B. (1955) *Symbolic Wounds: Puberty Rites and the Envious Male*, London: Thames and Hudson

Beyer, M. (1992) 'The Situation of East German Women in Post-unification Germany', *Women's Studies International Forum* 15, 1, pp. 111–14

Bischoff, C. et al. (eds) (1984) *FrauenKunstGeschichte. Zur Korrektur des herrschenden Blickes*, Giessen: Anabas

Bloch, E. (1977) 'Nonsynchronism and Dialectics', *New German Critique* 11, Spring, pp. 22–38 [Ger 1967]

Bock, G. (1986) *Zwangsterilisation im Nationalsozialismus. Studien zur Rassenpolitik und zur Frauenpolitik*, Opladen: Westdeutscher Verlag

Bock, G. and B. Duden (1976) 'Arbeit aus Liebe—Liebe als Arbeit. Zur Entstehung der Hausarbeit im Kapitalismus' in *Frauen und Wissenschaft. Beiträge zur Berliner Sommeruniversität für Frauen, Juli 1976*, Berlin: Courage, pp. 111–99

Boff, L. (1985) *Church, Charisma, and Power: Liberation Theology and the Institutional Church*, trans. J. W. Diercksmeier, New York: Crossroad [Portuguese 1981]

Böhme, G. and H. Böhme (1985) *Das Andere der Vernunft: Zur Entwicklung von Rationalitätsstrukturen am Beispiel Kants*, Frankfurt am Main: Suhrkamp

Bornemann, E. (1979) *Das Patriarchat. Ursprung und Zukunft unseres Gesellschaftssystems*, Frankfurt am Main: Fischer

Böttger, B. (1987) 'Macht und Liebe, Gleichberechtigung und Subsistenz—Kein Ort. Nirgends', *Beiträge zur feministischen Theorie und Praxis* 10, pp. 9–27

Böttger, B. et al. (1985) 'Grüne Parlamentarierinnen—Macht für Frauen?', *Beiträge zur feministischen Theorie und Praxis* 8, pp. 131–44

Bourdieu, P. (1990) 'Structures, *habitus*, practices' in *The Logic of Practice*, trans. R. Nice, Stanford, California: Stanford University Press

Bovenschen, S. (1978) 'The Contemporary Witch, the Historical Witch and the Witch Myth: The Witch, Subject of the Appropriation of Nature and Object of the Domination of Nature', trans. J. Blackwell et al., *New German Critique* 15, pp. 83–119 [Ger 1977]

—— (1979) *Die imaginierte Weiblichkeit*, Frankfurt am Main: Suhrkamp

—— (1985) 'Is There a Feminine Aesthetic?' in Ecker (ed.) *Feminist Aesthetics*, pp. 23–50 [Ger 1976]

Braun, C. v. (1985) *NICHT ICH. Logik, Lüge, Libido*, Frankfurt am Main: Neue Kritik

—— (1989) *Die schamlose Schönheit des Vergangenen. Zum Verhältnis von Geschlecht und Geschichte*, Frankfurt am Main: Neue Kritik

—— (1992) '"Der Jude" und "das Weib". Zwei Stereotypen des "Anderen" in der Moderne', *Metis* 1, 2, pp. 6–28

Breitling, G. (1985) 'Speech, Silence and the Discourse of Art: On Conventions of Speech and Feminine Consciousness' in Ecker (ed.) *Feminist Aesthetics*, pp. 162–74 [Ger 1983]

—— (1990) *Der verborgene Eros. Weiblichkeit und Männlichkeit im Zerrspiegel der Künste*, Frankfurt am Main: Fischer

Brick, B. (1992) 'Überlegungen zu Herbert Marcuses Begriff einer "mütterlichen Moral"' in Kulke and Scheich (eds) *Zwielicht der Vernunft*, pp. 165–72

Briffault, R. (1927) *The Mothers: A Study of the Origins of Sentiments and Institutions*, 3 vols, New York: Manhattan [Fr 1927]

Brinker-Gabler, B. (ed.) (1988) *Deutsche Literatur von Frauen*, 2 vols, Munich: Beck

Brockhaus, G. (1990) 'Opfer, Täterin, Mitbeteiligte. Zur Diskussion um die Rolle der Frauen im Nationalsozialismus' in Gravenhorst and Tatschmurat (eds) *Töchter-Fragen*, pp. 107–26

Bronfen, E. (1987) 'Die schöne Leiche. Weiblicher Tod als motivische Konstante von der Mitte des neunzehnten Jahrhunderts bis in die Moderne' in Berger and Stephan (eds) *Weiblichkeit und Tod in der Literatur*, pp. 87–115

—— (1992) *Over Her Dead Body: Death, Femininity and the Aesthetic*, Manchester: Manchester University Press [Ger 1993]

Brügmann, M. (1986) *Amazonen der Literatur. Studien zur deutschsprachigen Frauenliteratur der siebziger Jahre*, Amsterdam: Rodopi

Brügmann, M. and M. Kublitz-Kramer (eds) (1993) *Textdifferenzen und feministisches Engagement. Feminismus, Ideologiekritik, Poststrukturalismus*, Pfaffenweiler: Centaurus

Büchner, U. (1984) 'Frauenwissenschaft und Frauenstudien als radikale Wissenschaftskritik—dargestellt am Beispiel hochschuldidaktischer Praxis', *Beiträge zur feministischen Theorie und Praxis* 11, pp. 132–42

Butler, J. (1990) *Gender Trouble: Feminism and the Subversion of Identity*, New York: Routledge

Chodorow, N. (1978) *The Reproduction of Mothering: Psychoanalysis and the Sociology of Gender*, Berkeley: University of California Press

Christ, C. (1987) *Laughter of Aphrodite. Reflections on a Journey to the Goddess*, San Francisco: Harper and Row

Christadler, M. (ed.) (1990) *Freiheit, Gleichheit, Weiblichkeit. Aufklärung, Revolution und die Frauen in Europa*, Opladen: Leske and Budrich

Cixous, H. (1976) 'The Laugh of the Medusa', trans. K. Cohen and P. Cohen, *Signs* 1, pp. 245–64 [Fr 1975]

Cixous, H. and C. Clément (1986) *The Newly Born Woman*, trans. B. Wing, Minneapolis: University of Minnesota Press [Fr 1975]

Conrad, J. and U. Konnertz (eds) (1986) *Weiblichkeit in der Moderne. Ansätze feministischer Vernunftkritik*, vol. 1, Tübingen: edition diskord

Daele, W. v. d. (1988) 'Der Fötus als Subjekt und die Autonomie der Frau. Wissenschaftlich-technische Optionen und soziale Kontrollen in der Schwangerschaft' in U. Gerhardt and Y. Schütze (eds) *Frauensituation. Veränderungen in den letzten zwanzig Jahren*, Frankfurt am Main: Suhrkamp, pp. 189–218

Dalla Costa, M. and S. James (1975) *The Power of Women and the Subversion of the Community*, Bristol: Falling Wall Press

Daly, M. (1973) *Beyond God the Father: Toward a Philosophy of Women's Liberation*, Boston: Beacon Press

—— (1978) *Gyn/Ecology: The Metaethics of Radical Feminism*, Boston: Beacon Press

—— (1984) *Pure Lust: Elemental Feminist Philosophy*, Boston: Beacon Press

Decken, G. v. d. (1988a) *Emanzipation auf Abwegen. Frauenkultur und Frauenliteratur im Umkreis des Nationalsozialismus*, Frankfurt am Main: Hain

—— (1988b) 'Die neue Macht des Weibes' in Brinker-Gabler (ed.) *Deutsche Literatur von Frauen*, vol. 2, pp. 285–93

d'Eramo, L. (1988) 'Die Rhetorik der faschistischen Machtausübung oder: Opfern ist Macht' in Schaeffer-Hegel (ed.) *Frauen und Macht*, pp. 75–80

Deuber-Mankowsky, A. et al. (eds) (1989) *1789/1989 Die Revolution hat nicht stattgefunden. Dokumentation des V. Symposions der Internationalen Assoziation von Philosophinnen*, Tübingen: edition diskord

Diner, H. (alias Sir Galahad; b. Eckstein-Diener) (1932) *Mütter und*

Amazonen. Ein Umriß weiblicher Reiche, Munich: A. Langen

Diotima (eds) (1991) *Il pensiero della differenza sessuale*, Milan: La Tartaruga

Dölling, I. (1989) 'Culture and Gender' in M. Tueschemeyer and C. Lenke (eds) *The Quality of Life in the German Democratic Republic*, New York and London: M.E. Sharpe, pp. 27–47

Doormann, L. (1979) 'Die neue Frauenbewegung in der Bundesrepublik. Geschichte—Tendenzen—Perspektiven' in L. Doormann (ed.) *Keiner schiebt uns weg. Zwischenbilanz der Frauenbewegung in der Bundesrepublik*, Weinheim: Beltz, pp. 16–70

Dornhof, D. (1993) 'Weiblichkeit als Paradigma moderner Ästhetik? Überlegungen zu einer Begriffs- und Bedeutungsgeschichte von Weiblichkeit' in Brügmann and Kublitz-Kramer (eds) *Textdifferenzen und feministisches Engagement*, pp. 173–83

Duden, B. (1977) 'Das schöne Eigentum. Zur Herausbildung des bürgerlichen Frauenbildes an der Wende vom 18. zum 19. Jahrhundert', *Kursbuch* 47, pp. 125–40

—— (1991a) *The Woman Beneath the Skin: A Doctor's Patients in Eighteenth-Century Germany*, trans. T. Dunlop, Cambridge, Mass. and London: Harvard University Press [Ger 1987]

—— (1991b) *Der Frauenleib als öffentlicher Ort. Vom Mißbrauch des Begriffs Leben*, Darmstadt: Luchterhand

—— (1993) 'Die Frau ohne Unterleib: Zu Judith Butlers Entkörperung. Ein Zeitdokument', *Feministische Studien* 11, 2, pp. 24–33

Dux, G. (1992) *Die Spur der Macht im Verhältnis der Geschlechter. Über den Ursprung der Ungleichheit zwischen Frau und Mann*, Frankfurt am Main: Suhrkamp

Eckart, C. (1992) 'Rationalisierungszwang in weiblichen Biographien' in Kulke and Scheich (eds) *Zweilicht der Vernunft*, pp. 101–5

Ecker, G. (1985a) 'Poststrukturalismus und feministische Wissenschaft. Eine heimliche oder unheimliche Allianz?' in Berger et al. (eds) *Frauen, Weiblichkeit, Schrift*, pp. 8–20

—— (ed.) (1985b) *Feminist Aesthetics*, trans. H. Anderson, London: Women's Press

—— (1988) 'Spiel und Zorn. Zu einer feministischen Praxis der Dekonstruktion' in Pelz et al. (eds) *Frauen—Literatur—Politik*, pp. 8–22

—— (1993) 'Postscriptum 1992: Postmoderne und feministisches Engagement' in Brügmann and Kublitz-Kramer (eds) *Textdifferenzen und feministisches Engagement*, pp. 67–77

—— (1994a) *Differenzen. Essays zu Weiblichkeit und Kultur*, Dülmen-Hiddingsel: tende

—— (1994b) 'Mutter-Posen. Neue Blicke auf ein altes Motiv im Werk zeitgenössischer Künstlerinnen', in *Differenzen*, pp. 243–90

Edding, C. (1983) *Einbruch in den Herrenclub*, Reinbek: Rowohlt

Engels, F. (1972) *The Origin of the Family, Private Property and the State* [1884], intro. M. Barrett, Harmondsworth: Penguin

Erler, G. (1978) 'Einige—vielleicht gar nicht "feministische"—Anmerkungen zur Familienpolitik in der Bundesrepublik', *Beiträge zur feministischen Politik und Praxis*, 3, pp. 11–37

—— (1985) *Frauenzimmer. Für eine Politik des Unterschieds*, Berlin: Wagenbach

Erler, G. et al. (1988) 'Müttermanifest. Leben mit Kindern—Mütter werden laut', *Beiträge zur feministischen Theorie und Praxis* 11, pp. 201–7

Firestone, S. (1970) *The Dialectic of Sex: The Case for Feminist Revolution*, New York: Morrow

Fischer, E. (1989) 'Unfälle, die sich häufen. Lose Gedanken über Hoffnung, Revolution und Frauenmacht' in Nölle-Fischer (ed.) *Zukunft, gibt's die?*, pp. 67–79

Fischer, K. et al. (eds) (1992) *Bildersturm im Elfenbeinturm: Ansätze feministischer Literaturwissenschaft*, Tübingen: Attempto

Forschungsprojekt zur Geschichte der Theologinnen (eds) (1993) *Querdenken. Beiträge zur feministisch-befreiungstheologischen Diskussion*, Pfaffenweiler: Centaurus

Foucault, M. (1972) *The Archeology of Knowledge*, trans. A. M. Sheridan Smith, London: Tavistock [Fr 1969]

—— (1978) *The History of Sexuality. An Introduction*, trans. R. Hurley, New York: Pantheon [Fr 1976]

Francia, L. (1989) *Zaubergarn*, Munich: Frauenoffensive

Freier, H. (1976) *Die Rückkehr der Götter*, Stuttgart: Metzler

Freire, P. (1993) *Pedagogy of the Oppressed* (rev. edn), New York: Continuum

Freud, S. (1977) 'Female Sexuality' [1931], in *On Sexuality: Three Essays on the Theory of Sexuality, and Other Works*, trans. under the general editorship of J. Strachey, ed. A. Richards, Harmondsworth: Penguin, pp. 367–92

—— (1983) 'Femininity' [1932], in *New Introductory Lectures on Psychoanalysis*, trans. J. Strachey, ed. J. Strachey and A. Richards, London: Penguin, pp. 145–69

Gambaroff, M. et al. (eds) (1986) *Tschernobyl hat unser Leben verändert. Vom Ausstieg der Frauen*, Reinbek: Rowohlt

Gerhard, U. (1978) *Verhältnisse und Verhinderungen. Frauenarbeit, Familie und Rechte der Frauen im 19. Jahrhundert. Mit Dokumenten*, Frankfurt am Main: Suhrkamp

—— (as Gerhard-Teuscher) (1986) 'Die Frau als Rechtsperson. Über die Voreingenommenheit der Jurisprudenz als dogmatische Wissenschaft' in Hausen and Nowotny (eds) *Wie männlich ist die Wissenschaft?*, pp. 108–26

—— (1992) 'German Women's Studies and the Women's Movement:

A Portrait of Themes', trans. T. Levin, *Women's Studies Quarterly* 3/4, pp. 98–111

Gerhardt, M. (1986) *Stimmen und Rhythmen. Weibliche Ästhetick und Avantgarde*, Darmstadt: Luchterhand

Gilligan, C. (1982) *In a Different Voice: Psychological Theory and Women's Development, Cambridge, Mass.: Harvard University Press*

Gnüg, H. and R. Möhrmann (eds) (1985) *Frauen Literatur Geschichte. Schreibende Frauen vom Mittelalter bis zur Gegenwart*, Frankfurt am Main: Suhrkamp

Göttner-Abendroth, H. (1980) *Die Göttin und ihr Heros. Die matriarchalen Religionen in Mythos, Märchen und Dichtung*, Munich: Frauenoffensive

—— (1982) *Die tanzende Göttin. Prinzipien einer matriarchalen Aesthetik*, Munich: Frauenoffensive

—— (1985) 'Nine Principles of a Matriarchal Aesthetic' in Ecker (ed.) *Feminist Aesthetics*, pp. 81–94 [from Göttner-Abendroth (1982)]

—— (1988) *Das Matriarchat I. Geschichte seiner Erforschung*, Stuttgart, Berlin and Cologne: Kohlhammer

—— (1989) *Für die Musen. Neun Essays*, Frankfurt am Main: Campus

—— (1991a) *Das Matriarchat II, 1. Stammesgesellschaften in Ostasien, Indonesien, Ozeanien*, Stuttgart, Berlin and Cologne: Kohlhammer

—— (1991b) *The Dancing Goddess. Principles of a Matriarchal Aesthetics*, trans. M. T. Krause, Boston: Beacon

Gravenhorst, L. (1990) 'Nehmen wir Nationalsozialismus und Auschwitz ausreichend als unser negatives Eigentum in Anspruch? Zu Problemen im feministisch-sozialwissenschaftlichen Diskurs in der Bundesrepublik Deutschland' in Gravenhorst and Tatschmurat (eds) *Töchter-Fragen*, pp. 17–38

Gravenhorst, L. and C. Tatschmurat (eds) (1990) *Töchter-Fragen. NS-Frauen-Geschichte*, Freiburg im Breisgau: Kore

Graves, R. (1961) *The White Goddess: A Historical Grammar of Poetic Myth*, London and Boston: Faber

Grossmann, S. (1987) 'Schöpfer und Schöpfung in der feministischer Theologie' in Altner (ed.) *Ökologische Theologie*, pp. 213–33

Die GRÜNEN im Bundestag, AK Frauenpolitik (eds) (1987) *Frauen und Ökologie. Gegen den Machbarkeitswahn*, Cologne: Kölner Volksblatt

Gruppe feministische Öffentlichkeit (eds) (1992) *Femina Publica. Frauen—Öffentlichkeit—Feminismus*, Cologne: PapyRossa

Günther, S. and H. Kotthof (1991) 'Von fremden Stimmen. Weibliches und männliches Sprechen im Kulturvergleich' in Günther and Kotthof (eds) *Von fremden Stimmen*, Frankfurt am Main: Suhrkamp, pp. 7–51

Habermas, J. (1984) *The Theory of Communicative Action*, trans. T. McCarthy, Boston: Beacon Press [Ger 1981]

—— (1989) *The Structural Transformation of the Public Sphere: An Inquiry into a Category of Bourgeois Society*, trans. R. Burger and F. Lawrence, Cambridge, Mass.: MIT Press [Ger 1962]

Hacker, H. (1984) 'Von Frau zu Frau auf dem blanken Parkett der Meta-Ebene. Androzentrische Systematisierung und die Frage nach lesbischer Authentizität (Österreich 1870-1914)' in Bechtel et al. (eds) *Die ungeschriebene Geschichte*, pp. 151–60

Hagemann-White, C. (1984) 'Thesen zur kulturellen Konstruktion der Zweigeschlechtlichkeit' in Schaeffer-Hegel and Wartmann (eds) *Mythos Frau*, pp. 137–9

—— (1988) 'Wir werden nicht zweigeschlechtlich geboren . . .' in Hagemann-White and Rerrich (eds) *FrauenMännerBilder*, pp. 224–35

—— (1989) *Was heißt weiblich denken? Feministische Entwürfe einer anderen Vernunft, Antrittsvorlesung an der Universität Osnabrück, 24. Nov. 1988*, Osnabrück: Universität Osnabrück

Hagemann-White, C. and M. S. Rerrich (eds) (1988) *FrauenMänner-Bilder. Männer und Männlichkeit in der feministischen Diskussion*, Bielefeld: AJZ

Halkes, C. (1980) *Gott hat nicht nur starke Söhne*, Gütersloh: Gütersloher Verlagshaus

Hark, S. (1989) 'Eine Lesbe ist eine Lesbe, ist eine Lesbe . . . oder? Feminismus und Lesben in den 80ern?', *Beiträge zur feministischen Theorie und Praxis* 12, pp. 59–70

Hassauer, F. and P. Roos (1988) 'Aufklärung: Futurologie oder Konkurs? Acht Behauptungen' in Rüsen et al. (eds) *Die Zukunft der Aufklärung*, pp. 40–7

Haug, F. (1980) 'Opfer oder Täter? Über das Verhalten von Frauen', *Das Argument* 123, pp. 643–9

—— (1981) 'Männergeschichte, Frauenbefreiung, Sozialismus. Zum Verhältnis von Frauenbewegung und Arbeiterbewegung', *Das Argument* 129, pp. 649–64

—— (1984) 'Morals Also Have Two Genders', *New Left Review* 143, Jan.–Feb., pp. 51–68 [Ger 1983]

—— (1988) 'Mothers in the Fatherland', *New Left Review* 172, Nov.–Dec., pp. 105–15

—— (1990) *Erinnerungsarbeit*, Hamburg: Argument

—— (1992) *Beyond Female Masochism: Memory-Work and Politics*, trans. R. Livingstone, London and New York: Verso

Haug, F. et al. (1983) *Sexualisierung der Körper*, Berlin: Argument

Haug, F. et al. (1987) *Female Sexualisation. A Collective Work of Memory*, trans. E. Carter, London and New York: Verso

Haug, F. and K. Hauser (eds) (1985–86) *Kritische Psychologie der Frauen*, Berlin: Argument

—— (1991) *Die andere Angst*, Hamburg: Argument

Hausen, K. (1981) 'Family and Role-Division: The Polarisation of Sexual Stereotypes in the Nineteenth Century—an Aspect of the Dissociation of Work and Family Life' in L. Evans and W. R. Lee (eds) *The German Family*, London: Croom Helm, pp. 51–83 [Ger 1976]

Hausen, K. and H. Nowotny (eds) (1986) *Wie männlich ist die Wissenschaft?* Frankfurt am Main: Suhrkamp

Hauser, K. (1987) *Strukturwandel des Privaten? Das 'Geheimnis des Weibes' als Vergesellschaftungsrätsel*, Berlin: Argument

Haushofer, M. (1957) *Die Tapetentür*, Vienna: Zsolnay

—— (1958) *Wir töten Stella*, Vienna: Bergland

—— (1963) *Die Wand*, Gütersloh: Mohn

Heenen, S. (ed.) (1984) *Frauenstrategien*, Frankfurt am Main: Neue Kritik

Heine, S. (1988) *Christianity and the Goddesses: Systematic Criticism of a Feminist Theology*, London: SCM [Ger 1986]

Hering, H. (1991) 'Frauen in bester Verfassung. Das erste Jahr unserer Initiative in der Humanistischen Union', *Feministische Studien* 9, 1, pp. 97–103

Heschel, S. (1987) 'Interview', *Schlangenbrut* 16, pp. 6–9

—— (1988) 'Jüdisch-feministische Theologie und Antijudaismus in christlich-feministischer Theologie' in Siegele-Wenschkewitz (ed.) *Verdrängte Vergangenheit*, pp. 54–103

—— (1993) 'Altes Gift in neuen Schläuchen. Antijudaismus und Antipharisäismus in der christlich-feministischen Theologie' in Forschungsprojekt zur Geschichte der Theologinnen (eds) *Querdenken*, pp. 65–76

Heuser, M. (1983) 'Literatur von Frauen/Frauen in der Literatur. Feministische Literaturwissenschaft' in Pusch (ed.) *Feminismus*, pp. 117–48

Hippel, T. G. v. (1978) *Über die bürgerliche Verbesserung der Weiber* [1791], in *Sämtliche Werke*, vol. 6, Berlin and New York: Walter de Gruyter

—— (1979) *On Improving the Status of Women*, trans. and intro. T. F. Sellner, Detroit: Wayne University Press

Hoff, D. v. (1989) *Dramen des Weiblichen. Deutschsprachige Autorinnen um 1800*, Opladen: Westdeutscher Verlag

Honegger, C. (1978) 'Einleitung' in C. Honegger (ed.) (1978) *Die Hexen der Neuzeit. Studien zur Sozialgeschichte eines strukturellen Deutungsmusters*, Frankfurt am Main: Suhrkamp, pp. 21–151

—— (1984) 'Vorbemerkung' in Honegger and Heintz (eds) *Listen der Ohnmacht*, pp. 11–68

—— (1991) *Die Ordnung der Geschlechter. Die Wissenschaften vom Menschen und das Weib, 1750–1850*, Frankfurt am Main: Campus

Honegger, C. and B. Heintz (eds) (1984) *Listen der Ohnmacht*, Frankfurt am Main: Europäische Verlagsanstalt

Horney, K. (1967) *Feminine Psychology*, ed. and intro. H. Kelman, New York: Norton

Janetzky, B. et al. (eds) (1989) *Aufbruch der Frauen. Herausforderungen und Perspektiven feministischer Theologie*, Münster: Liberaci'on

Jansen, S. (1984) 'Magie und Technik. Auf der Suche nach feministischen Alternativen zur patriarchalen Naturnutzung', *Beiträge zur feministischen Theorie und Praxis* 12, pp. 69–84

Janssen-Jurreit, M. (1976) *Sexismus. Über die Abtreibung der Frauenfrage*, Frankfurt am Main: Fischer

—— (1982) *Sexism: The Male Monopoly on History and Thought*, abridged trans. V. Moberg, London: Pluto Press

Jay, M. (1973) *The Dialectical Imagination. A History of the Frankfurt School and the Institute of Social Research 1923–1950*, London: Heinemann

Jost, R. and U. Kubera (eds) (1991) *Befreiung hat viele Farben. Feministische Theologie als kontextuelle Befreiungstheologie*, Gütersloh: Gütersloher Verlagshaus

Kassel, M. (ed.) (1988) *Feministische Theologie. Perspektiven zur Orientierung*, Stuttgart: Kreuz

Kessler, S. J. and W. McKenna (1978) *Gender: An Ethnomethodological Approach*, New York: Wiley

Kliewer, A. (1987) 'Von deutscher Gottesmutterschaft. Mütterlichkeit als Maxime "weiblicher Moral"' in Schaumberger (ed.) *Weil wir nicht vergessen wollen*, pp. 59–72

—— (1992) 'Zur Flucht in den "gestaltlosen Urgrund". Matriarchat als "patriarchalisches Gepäck" der feministischen Theologie?', *Beiträge zur feministischen Theorie und Praxis* 32, pp. 107–16

Klinger, C. (1986) 'Modernisierungsorientiertes oder traditionorientiertes Emanzipationskonzept? Zwei Befreiungsbewegungen—Ein Dilemma' in Andreas-Grisebach and Weißhaupt (eds) *Was Philosophinnen denken*, pp. 71–96

Knapp, G.-A. (1987) 'Arbeitsteilung und Sozialisation: Konstellationen von Arbeitsvermögen und Arbeitskraft im Lebenszusammenhang von Frauen' in Beer (ed.) *Klasse Geschlecht*, pp. 267–308

—— (1988) 'Die vergessene Differenz', *Feministische Studien* 6, 1, pp. 12–31

—— (1991) 'Zur Theorie und politischen Utopie des "affidamento"', *Feministische Studien* 9, 1, pp. 117–27

—— (1992) 'Macht und Geschlecht. Neuere Entwicklungen in der feministischen Macht- und Herrschaftsdiskussion' in Knapp and Wetterer (eds) *Traditionen Brüche*, pp. 287–321

Knapp, G.-A. and A. Wetterer (eds) (1992) *Traditionen Brüche*.

Entwicklungen feministischer Theorie, Freiburg im Breisgau: Kore

Koedt, A. (1973) 'The Myth of Vaginal Orgasm' in Koedt et al. (eds) *Radical Feminism*, New York: Quadrangle, pp. 198–207

Konnertz, U. (ed.) (1988) *Zeiten der Keuschheit. Ansätze feministischer Vernunftkritik*, vol. 2, Tübingen: edition diskord

—— (ed.) (1989) *Weibliche Ängste. Ansätze feministischer Vernunftkritik*, vol. 3, Tübingen: edition diskord

—— (ed.) (1991) *Grenzen der Moral. Ansätze feministischer Vernunftkritik*, vol. 4, Tübingen: edition diskord

Koonz, C. (1987) *Mothers in the Fatherland: Women, the Family, and Nazi Politics*, London and New York: St Martin's Press

Kristeva, J. (1976a) *About Chinese Women*, trans. A. Barrows, London: Marion Boyars [Fr 1974]

—— (1976b) 'Produktivität der Frau: Interview von E. Bouquey' in *Das Lächeln der Medusa*, pp. 166–72

—— (1980) *Desire in Language: A Semiotic Approach to Literature and Art*, ed. L. S. Roudiez, trans. T. Gora, A. Jardine, L. S. Roudiez, Oxford: Basil Blackwell

—— (1984) *Revolution in Poetic Language*, trans. M. Waller, New York: Columbia University Press [Fr 1974]

—— (1991) *Strangers to Ourselves*, trans. L. S. Roudiez, New York: Columbia University Press [Fr 1987]

Krüger, M. (1987) 'Überlegungen und Thesen zu einer feministischen Sozial-Wissenschaft' in Beer (ed.) *Klasse Geschlecht*, pp. 67–94

Kublitz-Kramer, M. (1992) 'Literaturwissenschaftliche Frauenforschung und Literaturwissenschaft', *Mitteilungen des Deutschen Germanistenverbandes* 39, 3, pp. 41–6

Kulke, C. (ed.) (1988a) *Rationalität und sinnliche Vernunft. Frauen in der patriarchalischen Realität*, Pfaffenweiler: Centaurus

—— (1988b) 'Von der instrumentellen zur kommunikativen Rationalität patriarchaler Herrschaft' in Kulke (ed.) *Rationalität und Vernunft*, pp. 55–70

—— (1989) 'Die Logik patriarchaler Vernunftkritik. Ein weiblicher Zugriff auf die Dialektik der Aufklärung' in Deuber-Mankowsky et al. (eds) *1789/1989 Die Revolution hat nicht stattgefunden*, pp. 98–113

—— (1990) 'Die Politik instrumenteller Rationalität und die instrumentelle Rationalität von Politik—eine Dialektik des Geschlechtsverhältnisses' in Nagl-Docekal and Pauer-Studer (eds) *Denken der Geschlechterdifferenz*, pp. 71–87

Kulke, C. and E. Scheich (eds) (1992) *Zwielicht der Vernunft. Die Dialektik der Aufklärung aus der Sicht von Frauen*, Pfaffenweiler: Centaurus

Das Lächeln der Medusa. Frauenbewegung/Sprache/Psychoanalyse (1976), *alternative* 108/109 (special issue)

Landweer, H. (1990) *Das Märtyrinnenmodell. Zur diskursiven Erzeugung weiblicher Identität*, Pfaffenweiler: Centaurus
—— (1993) 'Kritik und Verteidigung der Kategorie Geschlecht. Wahrnehmung- und symbol-theoretische Überlegungen zur sex/ gender Unterscheidung', *Feministische Studien* 11, 2, pp. 34–43
Lang, R. (1989) *Frauenquoten. Der einen Freud, des anderen Leid*, Bonn: J. H. W. Dietz
Lauterbach, H. (1993) '"Energie" als religiöser Leitbegriff in der nachchristlichen Spirituellen Frauenbewegung der Gegenwart' in Appich et al. (eds) *Eine andere Tradition*, pp. 86–126
Lenk, E. (1985), 'The Self-reflecting Woman' in Ecker (ed.) *Feminist Aesthetics*, pp. 51–8 [Ger 1976]
Lerner, G. (1986) *The Creation of Patriarchy*, Oxford and New York: Oxford University Press
Lindemann, G. (1993) 'Wider die Verdrängung des Leibes aus der Geschlechtskonstruktion', *Feministische Studien* 11, 2, pp. 44–54
Lindhoff, L. (1995) *Einführung in die feministische Literaturtheorie*, Stuttgart: Metzler
Lindner, I. et al. (eds) (1989) *Blickwechsel. Konstruktionen von Männlichkeit und Weiblichkeit in Kunst und Kunstgeschichte*, Berlin: Reimer
Lipp, C. (1986) 'Katzenmusiken, Kravalle und "Weiberrevolution". Frauenpolitischer Protest der Revolutionsjahre' in C. Lipp et al. (eds) (1986) *Schimpfende Weiber und patriotische Jungfrauen: Frauen im Vormärz und in der Revolution 1848/49*, Moos: Elster, pp. 112–30
List, E. (1990) 'Theorieproduktion und Geschlechterpolitik. Prolegomena zu einer feministischen Theorie der Wissenschaften' in Nagl-Docekal and Pauer-Studer (eds) *Denken der Geschlechterdifferenz*, pp. 58–183
Lorey, I. (1993) 'Der Körper als Text und das aktuelle Selbst: Butler und Foucault', *Feministische Studien* 11, 2, pp. 10–23
Lyotard, J.-F. (1984) *The Postmodern Condition: A Report on Knowledge*, trans. F. Bennington and B. Massumi, Minneapolis: University of Minnesota Press [Fr 1979]
Mabry, H. (1974) *Unkraut ins Parlament. Die Bedeutung weiblicher parlamentarischer Arbeit für die Emanzipation der Frau*, Lollar über Giessen: Andreas Achenbach
—— (1977) 'Mit oder ohne Marx zum Feminismus?', *Der Feminist. Beiträge zur Theorie und Praxis* 2, 1, pp. 1–21
Maihofer, A. (1992) 'Rekonstruktion von Gilligans Thesen zu einer "weiblichen" Moralauffassung als Kritik herrschender Moral' in Kulke and Scheich (eds) *Zwielicht der Vernunft*, pp. 127–37
Malinowski, B. (1927) *Sex and Repression in Savage Society*, London: Routledge and Kegan Paul

Mamozai, M. (1990) *Komplizinnen*, Reinbek: Rowohlt

Marcuse, H. (1974) 'Marxism and Feminism', *Women's Studies* 2, pp. 279–88 [Ger 1975]

Maron, M. (1991) *Stille Zeile Sechs*, Frankfurt am Main: Fischer

Mayer, H. (1982) *Outsiders: A Study in Life and Letters*, trans. D. M. Sweet, Cambridge, Mass.: MIT Press [Ger 1975]

Meehan, J. (ed.) (1995) *Feminists Read Habermas: Gendering the Subject of Discourse*, New York: Routledge

Meier-Seethaler, C. (1988) *Ursprünge und Befreiungen. Die sexistischen Wurzeln der Kultur*, Frankfurt am Main: Fischer

Meyer, E. (1983) *Zählen und Erzählen. Für eine Semiotik des Weiblichen*, Vienna: Medusa

—— (1984a) *Versprechen*, Basel and Frankfurt am Main: Stroemfeld and Roter Stern

—— (1984b) 'Die Wörter und das Labyrinth' in *Versprechen*, pp. 47–57

—— (1989) *Autobiographie der Schrift*, Basel and Frankfurt am Main: Stroemfeld and Roter Stern

—— (1990) *Der Unterschied, der eine Umgebung schafft. Kybernetik— Psychoanalyse—Feminismus*, Vienna: Turia and Kant

Meyer zur Capellen, R. (1993) 'Die Hohe Frau im Minnesang und im Parzival. Ihre verborgene Funktion in einer Zeit sozialen Wandels' in Meyer zur Capellen et al. (eds) (1993) *Die Erhöhung der Frau. Psychoanalytische Untersuchungen zum Einfluß der Frau in einer sich transformierenden Gesellschaft*, Frankfurt am Main: Suhrkamp, pp. 23–144

Michard, C. and C. Viollet (1991) 'Sex and Gender in Linguistics. Fifteen years of Feminist Research in the United States and Germany', *Feminist Issues* 11, Spring, pp. 53–88

Mies, M. (1978) 'Methodische Postulate zur Frauenforschung— dargestellt am Beispiel der Gewalt gegen Frauen', *Beiträge zur feministischen Theorie und Praxis* 1, pp. 41–63

—— (1980) *Indian Women and Patriarchy: Conflicts and Dilemmas for Students and Working Women*, trans. S. K. Sarkar, New Delhi: Concept [Ger 1973]

—— (1982) *The Lace Makers of Narsarpur: Indian Housewives Produce for the World Market*, London: Zed

—— (1983) 'Subsistenzproduktion, Hausfrauisierung, Kolonisierung', *Beiträge zur feministischen Theorie und Praxis* 6, pp. 115–24

—— (1984) 'Frauenforschung oder feministische Forschung? Die Debatte um feministische Wissenschaft und Methodologie', *Beiträge zur feministischen Theorie und Praxis* 7, pp. 40–60

—— (1986) *Patriarchy and Accumulation on a World Scale: Women in the International Division of Labour*, London and New Jersey: Zed

—— (1992) *Wider die Industrialisierung des Lebens. Eine feministische*

Kritik der Gen- und Reproduktionstechnik, Pfaffenweiler: Centaurus

Mies, M. et al. (1986) *Indian Women in Subsistence and Agricultural Labour*, Geneva: International Labour Office

Mies, M. et al. (1988) *Women: The Last Colony*, London and New Jersey: Zed

Mies, M. and V. Shiva (1993) *Ecofeminism*, Halifax, Novia Scotia: Fernwood and London: Zed

Milan Women's Bookstore Collective (eds) (1990) *Sexual Difference: A Theory of Social-Symbolic Practice*, ed. T. de Lauretis, trans. T. de Lauretis and P. Cicogna, Bloomington: Indiana University Press

Millet, K. (1970) *Sexual Politics*, New York: Doubleday

Mitscherlich, M. (1983a) *Die friedfertige Frau*, Frankfurt am Main: Fischer

—— (1983b) 'Antisemitismus—eine Männerkrankheit?' in *Die friedfertige Frau*, pp. 148–60

—— (1987) *Die Zukunft ist Weiblich*, Interview with G. Weigner, Zurich: Pendo

Moltmann-Wendel, E. (1978) *Liberty, Equality, Sisterhood: On the Emancipation of Women in Church and Society*, trans. R. Gritsch, Philadelphia: Fortress [Ger 1977]

—— (1982) *The Women around Jesus: Reflections on Authentic Personhood*, trans. J. Bowden, London: SCM [Ger 1980]

—— (1986) *A Land Flowing with Milk and Honey: Perspectives on Feminist Theology*, trans. J. Bowden, London: SCM [Ger 1985]

—— (1989) *Wenn Gott und Körper sich begegnen. Feministische Perspektiven zur Leiblichkeit*, Gütersloh: Gütersloher Verlagshaus

—— (1994) *I am my Body: New Ways of Embodiment*, trans. J. Bowden, London: SCM [Ger 1994]

Mudry, A. (ed.) (1991) *Gute Nacht, Du Schöne: Autorinnen blicken zurück*, Frankfurt: Luchterhand

Mulack, C. (1984) *Maria—die geheime Göttin im Christentum*, Stuttgart: Kohlhammer

—— (1987) *Jesus—der Gesalbte der Frauen*, Stuttgart: Kohlhammer

—— (1993) 'Jesus, die Nazis und die Männer', *Publik-Forum* 4, 26 Feb., p. 21

Müller, H. (1984) 'Hamletmachine' in *Hamletmachine and other Texts for the Stage*, ed. and trans. C. Weber, New York: Performing Arts Journal Publications, pp. 49–58 [Ger 1977]

Nadig, M. (1985) 'Ethnopsychoanalyse und Feminismus—Grenzen und Möglichkeiten', *Feministische Studien* 3, 2, pp. 103–16

—— (1986) *Die verborgene Kultur der Frau. Ethnopsychoanalytische Gespräche mit Bäuerinnen in Mexiko*, Frankfurt am Main: Fischer

—— (1992) 'Der ethnologische Weg zur Erkenntnis. Das weibliche Subjekt in der feministischen Wissenschaft' in Knapp and Wetterer (eds) *Traditionen Brüche*, pp. 151–200

Nagl-Docekal, H. and H. Pauer-Studer (eds) (1990) *Denken der Geschlechterdifferenz. Neue Fragen und Perspektiven der feministischen Philosophie*, Vienna: Wiener Frauenverlag

Nicholson, L. (ed.) (1990) *Feminism/Postmodernism*, New York: Routledge

Nölle-Fischer, K. (ed.) (1989) *Zukunft, gibt's die? Feministische Visionen für die neunziger Jahre*, Munich: Frauenoffensive

Nölleke, B. (1985) *In alle Richtungen zugleich. Denkstrukturen von Frauen*, Munich: Frauenoffensive

Nunner-Winkler, G. (ed.) (1991) *Weibliche Moral. Die Kontroverse um eine geschlechtsspezifische Ethik*, Frankfurt am Main and New York: Campus

Offenbach, J. (1983) 'Feminismus—Heterosexualität—Homosexualität' in Pusch (ed.) *Feminismus*, pp. 210–32

Opitz, C. (1984a) 'Weibliche Biographien des 13. Jahrhunderts zwischen hagiographischer Topik und historiographischer Fragestellung' in Bechtel et al. (eds) *Die ungeschriebene Geschichte*, pp. 327–36

—— (ed.) (1984b) *Weiblichkeit oder Feminismus? Beiträge zur interdisziplinären Frauentagung in Konstanz, 1983*, Weingarten: Drumlin

Ortner, S. B. and H. Whitehead (1981) *Sexual Meanings: The Cultural Construction of Gender and Sexuality*, Cambridge and New York: Cambridge University Press

Ostner, I. and K. Lichtblau (1991) *Feministische Vernunftkritik. Anzätze und Traditionen*, Frankfurt am Main: Campus

Otto-Peters, L. (1986) 'Für Alle' [1847] in S. L. Cocalis (ed.) *The Defiant Muse: German Feminist Poems from the Middle Ages to the Present*, New York: The Feminist Press, pp. 54–8

Pahnke, D. (1989) 'Die Spur der weisen Frauen. Von der altgermanischen Zeit über die historischen Hexen hin zu den heutigen feministischen Hexen' in Janetzky et al. (eds) *Aufbruch der Frauen*, pp. 136–49

—— (1990) 'Die neuen Hexen. Spiritualität und Politik', *Schlangenbrut* 30, Aug., pp. 8–14

—— (1992) *Ethik und Geschlecht. Menschenbild und Religion im Patriarchat und Feminismus*, Marburg: Diagonal

Pelz, A. et al. (eds) (1988) *Frauen—Literatur—Politik*, Berlin: Argument

Pfäfflin, U. (1988), 'Spiritualität und Psychologie' in Kassel (ed.) *Feministische Theologie*, pp. 137–64

Pissarek-Huderlist, H. and L. Schottroff (eds) (1991) *'Mit allen Sinnen glauben'. Feministische Theologie unterwegs*, Gütersloh: Gütersloher Verlagshaus

Plaskow, J. (1990) *Standing Again at Sinai: Judaism from a Feminist Perspective*, San Francisco: Harper

Prokop, U. (1978) 'Production and the Context of Women's Daily Life', *New German Critique* 13, Winter, pp. 18–33 [Ger 1976]

—— (1984) 'Der Mythos des Weiblichen und die Idee der Gleichheit in literarischen Entwürfen des frühen Bürgertums' in Stephan and Weigel (eds) *Feministische Literaturwissenschaft*, pp. 15–22

Pusch, L. (ed.) (1983) *Feminismus. Inspektion der Herrenkultur. Ein Handbuch*, Frankfurt am Main: Suhrkamp

—— (1984) *Das Deutsche als Männersprache*, Frankfurt am Main: Suhrkamp

Rang, B. (1986) 'Zur Geschichte des dualistischen Denkens über Mann und Frau. Kritische Anmerkungen zu den Thesen von Karin Hausen zur Herausbildung der Geschlechtscharaktere im achtzehnten und neunzehnten Jahrhundert' in J. Dalhoff et al. (eds) (1986) *Frauenmacht in der Geschichte. Beiträge des Historikerinnentreffens 1985 zur Frauengeschichtsforschung*, Düsseldorf: Schwann, pp. 194–204

Reese, D. and C. Sachse (1990) 'Frauenforschung und National-sozialismus. Eine Bilanz' in Gravenhorst and Tatschmurat (eds) *Töchter-Fragen*, pp. 73–106

Rentmeister, C. (1985) *Frauenwelten—Männerwelten. Für eine neue kulturpolitische Bildung*, Opladen: Leske and Budrich

Reuter, R. R. (1983) *Sexism and God-Talk: Toward a Feminist Theology*, Boston: Beacon Press

Rhode-Dachser, C. (1991a) *Expeditionen in den dunklen Kontinent. Weiblichkeit im Diskurs der Psychoanalyse*, Munich, Berlin and New York: Springer

—— (1991b) 'Das Bild der Mutter in der Psychoanalyse', in Verein Sozialwissenschaftliche Forschung und Bildung für Frauen— SFBF (ed.) *Körper—Bild—Sprache*, Frankfurt am Main: Selbstverlag, pp. 43–62

Richter, H. E. (1979) *Der Gotteskomplex. Die Geburt und die Krise des Glaubens an die Allmacht des Menschen*, Reinbek: Rowohlt

Richter-Schröder, K. (1986) *Frauenliteratur und weibliche Identität: Theoretische Ansätze zur Entwicklung der neuen deutschen Frauenliteratur*, Frankfurt am Main: Anton Hain

—— (1992) 'Feministischer Fort-Schritt? Weibliche Ästhetik und poststrukturalistische Literaturtheorie', in Fischer et al. (eds) *Bildersturm im Elfenbeinturm*, pp. 48–65

Rieger, E. (1985) '*Dolce semplice*'? On the Changing Role of Women in Music' in Ecker (ed.) *Feminist Aesthetics*, pp. 135–49 [Ger 1980]

Rothe, V. (1990) 'Die Auswirkung der Menschenrechtsdiskussion auf die deutsche Frauenbewegung' in Christadler (ed.) *Freiheit, Gleichheit, Weiblichkeit*, pp. 141–53

Rübsamen, R. (1983) 'Patriarchat—der (un-)heimliche Inhalt der Naturwissenschaft und Technik', in Pusch (ed.) *Feminismus*, pp. 290–307

Rumpf, M. (1989) *Spuren des Mütterlichen. Die widersprüchliche Bedeutung der Mutterrolle für die männliche Identitätsbildung in Kritischer Theorie und Feministischer Wissenschaft*, Frankfurt an Main and Hannover: Materialis

—— (1992) 'Das "moralische Gefühl". Zur Frage der Aktualität von Max Horkheimers Moralkritik' in Kulke and Scheich (eds) *Zwielicht der Vernunft*, pp. 155–63

Rüsen, J. et al. (eds) (1988) *Die Zukunft der Aufklärung*, Frankfurt am Main: Suhrkamp

Schaeffer-Hegel, B. (ed.) (1988) *Frauen und Macht. Der alltägliche Beitrag der Frauen zur Politik des Patriarchats*, Berlin: Pfaffenweiler [1984]

—— (1989) 'Die Freiheit und Gleichheit der Brüder. Weiblichkeitsmythos und Menschenrechte im politischen Diskurs um 1789' in Deuber-Mankowsky et al. (eds) *1789/1989 Die Revolution hat nicht stattgefunden*, pp. 51–64

—— (1992) 'Makers and Victims of Unification: German Women and the Two Germanies', *Women's Studies International Forum* 15, pp. 101–10

Schaeffer-Hegel, B. and B. Wartmann (eds) (1984) *Mythos Frau. Proketionen und Inszenierungen im Patriarchat*, Berlin: Publica-Verlagsgesellschaft [1980]

Schaumberger, C. (ed.) (1987) *Weil wir nicht vergessen wollen . . . Zu einer Feministischen Theologie im deutschen Kontext, AnFragen 1: Diskussionen Feministischer Theologie*, Münster: Morgana

—— (1991) '"Es geht um jede Minute unseres Lebens". Auf dem Weg zu einer kontextuellen feministischen Befreiungstheologie' in Jost and Kubera (eds) *Befreiung hat viele Farben*, pp. 15–34

Schaumberger, C. and L. Schottroff (eds) (1988) *Schuld und Macht. Studien zu einer feministischen Befreiungstheorie*, Munich: Kaiser

—— (1992) 'Feministische Befreiungstheologie' in Wetterer (ed.) *Frauenforschung*, pp. 49–80

Scheich, E. (1987) 'Frauen-Sicht. Zur politischen Theorie der Technik' in Beer (ed.) *Klasse Geschlecht*, pp. 132–61

—— (1988) 'Denkverbote über Frau und Natur—Zu den strukturellen Verdrängungen des naturwissenschaftlichen Denkens' in Kulke (ed.) *Rationalität und sinnliche Vernunft*, pp. 72–89

—— (1993) *Naturbeherrschung und Weiblichkeit. Denkformen und Phantasmen der modernen Naturwissenschaften*, Pfaffenweiler: Centaurus

Schenk, H. (1980) *Die feministische Herausforderung. 150 Jahre Frauenbewegung in Deutschland*, Munich: Beck [1977]

—— (1983) *Frauen kommen ohne Waffen. Feminismus und Pazifismus*, Berlin: Beck [1980]

Scherzberg, L. (1992) 'Die Göttin—Anachronismus oder Utopie? Über die Verwandtschaft des postchristlichen Feminismus mit der Romantik', *Schlangenbrut* 36, Feb., pp. 13–15

Schiran, U. M. (1988) *Menschenfrauen fliegen wieder. Die Jahreskreisfeste als weiblicher Initiationsweg*, Munich: Droemer Knaur

Schissler, H. (1990) 'Natur oder soziales Konstrukt? Zum Verhältnis der Geschlechter zwischen bürgerlichen Emanzipationsbewegungen und industrieller Gesellschaft' in Christadler (ed.) *Freiheit, Gleichheit, Weiblichkeit*, pp. 155–68

Schlaffer, H. (1994) 'Die Emanzipation der Männer', *Neue Rundschau* 105, 3, pp. 129–36

Schlesier, R. (1984) 'Die totgesagte Vagina. Zum Verhältnis von Psychoanalyse und Feminismus. Eine Trauerarbeit' in Schaeffer-Hegel and Wartmann (eds) *Mythos Frau*, pp. 111–33

—— (1990) *Mythos und Weiblichkeit bei Sigmund Freud. Zum Problem von Entmytholisierung und Remythologisierung in der psychoanalytischen Theorie*, Frankfurt am Main: Hain [1981]

Schlüpmann, H. (1990) 'Femininity as Productive Force: Kluge and Critical Theory', *New German Critique* 49, pp. 69–78

Schopenhauer, A. (1974) 'On Women' [1851], in *Parerga and Paralipomena: Short Philosophical Essays*, vol. 2, trans. E. F. J. Payne, Oxford: Clarendon Press, pp. 614–26

Schottroff, L. (1986) 'Die Partialität Gottes' in Gambaroff et al. (eds) *Tschernobyl hat unser Leben verändert*, pp. 137–44

—— (1987) 'Schöpfung im Neuen Testament' in Altner (ed.) *Ökologische Theologie*, pp. 130–48

—— (1991) 'Mit Händen und Füßen glauben' in Pissarek-Huderlist and Schottroff (eds) *'Mit allen Sinnen glauben'*, pp. 65–77

Schubert, H. (1990) *Judasfrauen. Zehn Fallgeschichten weiblicher Denunziation im 'Dritten Reich'*, Frankfurt am Main: Luchterhand

Schulenburg, A. (1993) *Feministische Spiritualität. Exodus in eine befreiende Kirche?*, Stuttgart: Kohlhammer

Schuller, M. (1979) 'Die Nachtseite der Humanwissenschaften, einige Aspekte zum Verhältnis Frauen und Literaturwissenschaft' in G. Dietze (ed.) *Die Überwindung der Sprachlosigkeit. Texte aus der neuen Frauenbewegung*, Darmstadt: Luchterhand, pp. 31–50

—— (1990a) *Im Unterschied. Lesen/Korrespondieren/Adressieren*, Frankfurt am Main: Neue Kritik

—— (1990b) 'Literarische Szenarien und ihre Schatten. Orte des "Weiblichen" in literarischen Produktionen' [1979] in *Im Unterschied*, pp. 47–66

—— (1990c) 'Sabine Spielrein lesen' [1988] in *Im Unterschied*, pp. 95–107 (1988)

—— (1990d) 'Vergabe des Wissens. Notizen zum Verhältnis von "weiblicher Intellektualität" und Macht' [1984] in *Im Unterschied*, pp. 189–98

—— (1990e) 'Wie entsteht weibliche Freiheit? Zur "neuen Politik" des Affidamento' [1989] in *Im Unterschied*, pp. 211–18

Schulz, I. (1992) 'Julie und Juliette und die Nachtseite der Geschichte Europas. Naturwissen, Aufklärung und pathetische Projektion in der "Dialektik der Aufklärung" von Adorno und Horkheimer' in Kulke and Scheich (eds) *Zwielicht der Vernunft*, pp. 25–40

Schüssler-Fiorenza, E. (1984) *In Memory of Her: A Feminist Theological Reconstruction of Christian Origins*, New York: Crossroad

Schwarzer, A. (1977) *Der kleine Unterschied und seine großen Folgen*, rev. edn, Frankfurt am Main: Fischer

—— (1986) (ed.) *Weg mit dem Par. 218*, Cologne: Emma

—— (1992) *Krieg. Was Männerwahn anrichtet und wie Frauen Widerstand leisten*, Frankfurt am Main: Fischer

Sichtermann, B. (1981) *Leben mit einem Neugeborenen: Ein Blick über das erste halbe Jahr*, Frankfurt am Main: Fischer

—— (1982) *Vorsicht, Kind: Eine Arbeitsplatzbeschreibung für Mütter, Väter u.a.*, [West] Berlin: Wagenbach

—— (1986) *Femininity. The Politics of the Personal*, trans. J. Whitlam, ed. H. Geyer-Ryan, Cambridge: Polity [Ger 1983]

—— (1987) *Wer ist wie? Über den Unterschied der Geschlechter*, [West] Berlin: Wagenbach

Siegele-Wenschkewitz, L. (ed.) (1988) *Verdrängte Vergangenheit, die uns bedrängt. Feministische Theologie in der Verantwortung für die Geschichte*, Munich: Kaiser

—— (1993) 'Rassismus, Antisemitismus und Sexismus', *Schlangenbrut* 43, pp. 15–18

Singer, M. (1988) 'Wider die Widerbelebung der Sinne in kleingärtnerischer Absicht' in Konnertz (ed.) *Zeiten der Keuschheit*, pp. 111–26

—— (1991) 'Über die Moral und die Grenzen des Verstehens' in Konnertz (ed.) *Grenzen der Moral*, pp. 159–79

Sölle, D., (1983) 'Gott und ihre Freunde: Zur feministischen Theologie' in Pusch (ed.) *Feminismus*, pp. 169–209

—— (1984) *To Love and to Work: A Theology of Creation*, with S. A. Cloyes, Philadelphia: Fortress [Ger 1985]

—— (1991a) 'Das Sakrament gegen die Zertrennungen' in Pissarek-Huderlist and Schottroff (eds) *'Mit allen Sinnen glauben'*, pp. 78–83

—— (1991b) *'Mitleiden—Mithandeln. Frauen unterweges zu der Einen Welt' in Jost and Kubera (eds)* Befreiung hat viele Farben, *pp. 63–77*

—— (1992) *Das Recht auf ein anderes Glück*, Stuttgart: Kreuz

Sorge, E. (1986) *Religion und Frau. Weibliche Spiritualität im Christentum*, Stuttgart: Kohlhammer

Starhawk [Miriam Simos] (1982) *Dreaming the Dark: Magic, Sex, and Politics*, Boston: Beacon Press
—— (1987) *Truth or Dare: Encounters with Power, Authority and Magic*, San Francisco: Harper and Row
—— (1989) *The Spiral Dance: A Rebirth of the Ancient Religion of the Goddess*, 10th anniversary edn, rev., San Francisco: Harper and Row
Stefan, V. (1979) *Shedding*, trans. J. Moore and B. Weckmuller, London: The Women's Press [Ger 1975]
Steinbrügge, L. (1987) *Das moralische Geschlecht. Theorien und literarische Entwürfe über die Natur der Frau in der französischen Aufklärung*, Ergebnisse der Frauenforschung, vol. 11, Weinheim-Basel: Metzler
—— (1989) 'Vernunftkritik und Weiblichkeit in der französischen Aufklärung' in Deuber-Mankowsky et al. (eds) *1789/1989 Die Revolution hat nicht stattgefunden*, pp. 65–79
Stephan, I. (1983a) '"Bilder, immer wieder Bilder . . ." Überlegungen zur Untersuchung von Frauenbildern in männlicher Literatur' in Stephan and Weigel (eds) *Die verborgene Frau*, pp. 15–34
—— (1983b) 'Hexe oder Heilige? zur Geschichte der Jeanne d'Arc und ihre literarische Bearbeitung' in Stephan and Weigel (eds) *Die verborgene Frau*, pp. 35–66
—— (1984) '"Da werden Weiber zu Hyänen . . ." Amazonen und Amazonenmythen bei Schiller und Kleist' in Stephan and Weigel (eds) *Feministische Literaturwissenschaft*, pp. 23–42
—— (1992) *Die Gründerinnen der Psychoanalyse*, Stuttgart: Kreuz
Stephan, I. and S. Weigel (eds) (1983) *Die verborgene Frau. Sechs Beiträge zu einer feministischen Literaturwissenschaft*, Berlin: Argument
—— (eds) (1984) *Feministische Literaturwissenschaft. Dokumentation der Tagung im Hamburg, Mai 1983*, Berlin: Argument
—— (eds) (1989) *Die Marsaillaise der Weiber. Frauen, die Französische Revolution und ihre Rezeption*, Berlin: Argument
Stephan, I. et al. (eds) (1991) *"Wen kümmert's, wer spricht?" Zur Literatur- und Kulturgeschichte von Frauen aus Ost und West*, Cologne and Vienna: Böhlau
Stopczyk, A. (1986) 'Vom Ausstieg aus der männlichen Zivilisation' in Gambaroff et al. (eds) *Tschernobyl hat unser Leben verändert*, pp. 188–203
—— (1988) 'Welche Bewegung macht das Leben?', *Tageszeitung* [Westberlin], 30 July 1988, p. 9
—— (1991) 'Leibphilosophie—eine sechsteilige Sendereihe beim Süddeutschen Rundfunk' [radio broadcast], March–April 1991
Stuby, A. M. (1992) *Liebe, Tod und Wasserfrau. Mythen des Weiblichen in der Literatur*, Opladen: Westdeutscher Verlag

Thürmer-Rohr, C. (1991) *Vagabonding: Feminist Thinking Cut Loose*, trans. L. Weil, Cambridge: Polity [Ger 1987]

Trömel-Plötz, S. (1982) *Frauensprache: Sprache der Veränderung*, Frankfurt am Main: Fischer

—— (ed.) (1984) *Gewalt durch Sprache. Die Vergewaltigung von Frauen in Gesprächen*, Frankfurt am Main: Fischer

Vaerting, M. (1975) *Die weibliche Eigenart im Männerstaat und die männliche Eigenart im Frauenstaat*, Berlin: Frauenselbstverlag [1921]

Vedder-Shults, N. (1978) 'Hearts Starve as Well as Bodies: Ulrike Prokop's "Production and the Context of Women's Daily Life"', *New German Critique* 13, Winter, pp. 5–17

Venske, R. (1988) *Mannsbilder—Männerbilder. Konstruktion und Kritik des Männlichen in zeitgenössischer deutschsprachiger Literatur von Frauen*, Hildesheim: Olms

Voss, J. (1988) *Das Scharzmondtabu*, Stuttgart: Kreuz

Wacker, M.-T. (ed.) (1987a) *Der Gott der Männer und die Frauen*, Düsseldorf: Patmos

—— (1987b) 'Die Göttin kehrt zurück. Kritische Sichtung neuerer Entwürfe' in Wacker (ed.) *Der Gott der Männer und die Frauen*, pp. 11–37

—— (ed.) (1988a) *Theologie feministisch*, Düsseldorf: Patmos

—— (1988b) 'Gefährliche Erinnerungen. Feministische Blicke auf die hebräische Bibel' in Wacker (ed.) *Theologie feministisch*, pp. 14–58

Wagner, B. (1982) *Zwischen Mythos und Realität. Die Frau in der frühgriechischen Gesellschaft*, Frankfurt am Main: Haag and Herchen

—— (as Wagner-Hasel) (1991) 'Das Matriarchat und die Krise der Modernität', *Feministische Studien* 9, 9, pp. 80–95

—— (as Wagner-Hasel) (1993) 'Umkehrprojektionen und das Bild der Moderne im Matriarchat', *Schlangenbrut* 42, pp. 7–10

Walser, K. (1984) 'Frauen als Opfer' in Heenan (ed.) *Frauenstrategien*, pp. 49–64

—— (as Windaus-Walser) (1990) 'Frauen im Nationalsozialismus. Eine Herausforderung für feministische Theoriebildung' in Gravenhorst and Tatschmurat (eds) *Töchter-Fragen*, pp. 59–72

Wartmann, B. (1984) 'Verdrängungen der Weiblichkeit aus der Geschichte. Bemerkungen zu einer "anderen" Produktivität der Frauen' in Schaeffer-Hegel and Wartmann (eds) *Mythos Frau*, pp. 7–33

Weigel, S. (1983a) 'Wider die romantische Mode. Zur ästhetischen Funktion des Weiblichen in Friedrich Schlegels *Lucinde*' in Stephan and Weigel (eds) *Die verborgene Frau*, pp. 67–82

—— (1983b) 'Der schielende Blick. Thesen zur Geschichte weiblicher

Schreibpraxis' in Stephan and Weigel (eds) *Die verborgene Frau*, pp. 83–137

——— (1984) 'Frau und "Weiblichkeit"—Theoretische Überlegungen zur feministischen Literaturkritik' in Stephan and Weigel (eds) *Feministische Literaturwissenschaft*, pp. 103–13

——— (1985) 'Double Focus: On the History of Women's Writing' [abridged trans. of 'Der schielende Blick'] in Ecker (ed.) *Feminist Aesthetics*, pp. 59–80

——— (1987a) *Die Stimme der Medusa. Schreibweisen in der Gegenwartsliteratur von Frauen*, Dülmen-Hiddingsel: Tende

——— (1987b) 'Die nahe Fremde—das Territorium des "Weiblichen". Zum Verhältnis von "Wilden" und "Frauen" im Diskurs der Aufklärung' in T. Koebner and G. Pickerodt (eds), *Die andere Welt. Studien zum Exotismus*, Frankfurt am Main: Athenaum, pp. 171–99

——— (1990a) *Topographien der Geschlechter. Kulturgeschichtliche Studien zu Literatur*, Hamburg: Rowohlt

——— (1990b) 'Body and Image Space: Problems and Representations of a Female Dialectic of Enlightenment' in A. Milner and C. Worth (eds) *Discourse and Difference. Poststructuralism, Feminism and the Moment of History*, Monash University, Melbourne: Centre for General and Comparative Literature, pp. 107–26 [Ger 1990]

——— (ed.) (1992) *Leib- und Bildraum. Lektüren nach Benjamin*, Cologne: Böhlau

——— (1994) *Bilder des kulturellen Gedächtnisses. Beiträge zur Gegenwartsliteratur*, Dülmen-Hiddingsel: tende

——— (ed.) (1995) *Flaschenpost und Postkarte. Korrespondenzen zwischen Kritischer Theorie und Poststrukturalismus*, Cologne, Weimar and Vienna: Böhlau

Weiler, G. (1984) *Ich verwerfe im Lande die Kriege. Das verborgene Matriarchat im Alten Testament*, Munich: Frauenoffensive

——— (1987) Reply to S. Heschel in *Schlangenbrut* 17, p. 21

——— (1989) *Das Matriarchat im alten Israel*, Stuttgart: Kohlhammer

——— (1990) *Ich brauche die Göttin. Zur Kulturgeschichte eines Symbols*, Basel: Mond-Buch

Weißhaupt, B. (1983) 'Sisyphos ohne Pathos. Selbsterhaltung und Selbstbestimmung im Alltag' in Bendkowsky and Weißhaupt (eds) *Was Philosophinnen denken*, pp. 271–90

——— (1986a) 'Dissidenz als Aufklärung. Elemente feministischer Wissenschaftskritik' in Andreas-Grisebach and Weißhaupt (eds) *Was Philosophinnen denken*, pp. 9–19

——— (1986b) 'Selbstlosigkeit und Wissen' in Conrad and Konnertz (eds) *Weiblichkeit in der Moderne*, pp. 21–38

——— (1989) 'Schatten des Geschlechts über der Vernunft' in Deuber-

Mankowsky et al. (eds) *1789/1989 Die Revolution hat nicht stattgefunden*, pp. 290–302

—— (1990) 'Schatten über der Vernunft' in Nagl-Docekal and Pauer-Studer (eds) *Denken der Geschlechterdifferenz*, pp. 136–57

—— (1991) 'Ethik und Technologie am Lebendigen' in Konnertz (ed.) *Grenzen der Moral*, pp. 75–92

Wenk, S. (1989) 'Pygmalions Wahlverwandtschaften. Die Rekonstruktion des Schöpfermythos im nachfaschistischen Deutschland' in Lindner et al. (eds) *Blickwechsel*, pp. 59–82

Werlhof, C. v. (1986), 'Wir werden das Leben unserer Kinder nicht dem Fortschritt opfern' in Gambaroff et al. (eds) *Tschernobyl hat unser Leben verändert*, pp. 8–24

Wetterer, A. (ed.) (1992) *Frauenforschung. Ergebnisse und Perspektiven an der Gesamthochschule Kassel*, Kassel: Jenior and Pressler

Wetterer, A. and B. Robak (1992) 'Arbeit und Beruf von Frauen' in Wetterer (ed.) *Frauenforschung*, pp. 165–221

Wiggershaus, R. (1994) *The Frankfurt School: Its History, Theories, and Political Significance*, trans. M. Robertson, Cambridge, Mass.: MIT Press [Ger 1986]

Wilson, W. D. and R. C. Holub (eds) (1993) *Impure Reason: Dialectic of Enlightenment in Germany*, Detroit: Wayne State University Press

Windaus-Walser, *see* Walser

Wisselinck, E. (1987) 'Über Politik und Spiritualität oder: Wenn Frauen Tabus brechen' in H. Mirus and E. Wisselinck (eds) *Mit Mut und Phantasie. Frauen suchen ihre verlorene Geschichte—eine Dokumentation*, Straßlach: Sophia, pp. 266–72

Wittrock, C. (1983) *Weiblichkeitsmythen. Das Frauenbild im Faschismus und seine Vorläufer in der Frauenbewegung der 20er Jahre*, Frankfurt am Main: Sendler

Woesler de Panafieu, C. (1987) 'Feministische Kritik am wissenschaftlichen Androzentrismus' in Beer (ed.) *Klasse Geschlecht*, pp. 95–131

Yeatman, A. (1990), 'A Feminist Theory of Social Differentiation' in Nicholson (ed.) *Feminism/Postmodernism*, pp. 281–99

Young, I. M. (1990) 'The Idea of Community and the Politics of Difference' in Nicholson (ed.) *Feminism/Postmodernism*, pp. 300–23

Index

Other Interpretations titles available from Melbourne University Press:

After a Fashion
JOANNE FINKELSTEIN

Commentators and theorists have variously seen fashion as a social, economic or aesthetic force, or sometimes as all three at once. Fashion seems to be novel but at the same time it preserves the status quo: it makes us think that change is occurring when the opposite is closer to the truth. Drawing on psychology, art, commerce and history, Joanne Finkelstein considers the different sides of this hybrid phenomenon, investigating fashion as body decoration and costume, as a language and form of irrational play, as an expression of sexuality and as part of the urban experience.

After Mabo
Interpreting indigenous traditions
TIM ROWSE

Many non-Aboriginal Australians, sensitive to the fact that their nation came into existence through the conquest and dispossession of indigenous peoples, continue to seek ways of righting historical wrongs. A significant stage was reached in the High Court's so-called Mabo decision of June 1992, which recognised a 'native right in land'. Tim Rowse draws on history, political science, anthropology, cultural studies, ecology and archaeology to critique non-Aboriginal ways of perceiving Aboriginality. He focuses on the moral and legal traditions of settlers and indigenous peoples, their different attitudes towards the environment, the institutional heritage of 'Aboriginal welfare', tensions between indigenous cultures and indigenous politics, and the representation of Aboriginal identities by Aboriginal writers.

> '*a stylish and shrewd book . . . should be read by all who try to follow Mabo*' Barry Hill, Age

The Architecture of Babel
Discourses of literature and science
DAMIEN BRODERICK

Today the humanities seem painfully severed from the sciences. Writers, artists and ordinary thinking citizens cannot readily understand the sciences that have reshaped modern life. Scientists in turn find critical theory difficult and elusive. Drawing on recent semiotic and post-structural approaches to the text, Damien Broderick provides a critical introduction to recent efforts to construct an interdisciplinary analysis of the 'two cultures', literature and science. He finds literary theorists deficient in scientific rigour, and would like scientists to acquire the linguistic sophistication of humanists and their postmodern successors. Both literary theories and scientific practices, he concludes, are deeply implicated in social contexts.

> '*an intriguing intellectual tour through exciting territory, much of which is at the cutting edge of literary and scientific philosophy*' Robyn Arianrhod, Age

The Body in the Text

ANNE CRANNY-FRANCIS

Male/female, white/black, mind/body: these fundamental distinctions, based on the way we see ourselves and others, face irrevocable breakdown as we stand on the edge of revolutions in artificial intelligence, robotics and genetic engineering. Cranny-Francis gives a lucid and stylish introduction to the ways in which the body is represented in our culture. Her clear, considered analysis shows how these representations are used as critiques of contemporary society by writers on gender, sexuality, race and class, and describes how these representations have changed the relationships between our understandings of the body and the ways in which we live and think about our world.

Cultural Materialism

ANDREW MILNER

For much of this century, idealist accounts sought to represent culture as 'pure' consciousness, while materialist accounts represented it as a secondary 'effect' of some other material reality. But from the 1970s new theoretical paradigms have attempted to establish the materiality of culture itself. This book is both an introduction and a contribution to cultural theory. It situates cultural materialism in relation to earlier paradigms such as literary humanism and Marxism, explains how it has been applied in such areas as cultural, media and literary studies, and explores the differences between British and French variants created by Raymond Williams, E. P. Thompson, Pierre Bourdieu and Michel Foucault.

> 'The accomplishments of Cultural Materialism are substantial . . . Milner's work achieves considerably more than the definition of a literary theory'
> Noel Henricksen, Australian Left Review

Debating Derrida

NIALL LUCY

'There is nothing outside the text.' Possibly no single statement has caused such a storm in critical theory as this famous observation by the French philosopher, Jacques Derrida. While it is often misunderstood as meaning that nothing is real, Debating Derrida demonstrates that Derrida's philosophy does not lack political conviction.

Niall Lucy examines three key terms—text, writing and différance—as they are used in three famous debates: Derrida's disputes over speech-acts with John R. Searle, over discourse with Michel Foucault and over apartheid. Lucy also takes up the issue of Derrida's relationship to postmodernism. Debating Derrida decisively shows that instead of disagreeing with Derrida, we should rather be defending him.

A Foucault Primer

Discourse, power and the subject

ALEC McHOUL AND WENDY GRACE

The French historian and philosopher, Michel Foucault, has had a profound influence on scholars in the humanities and social sciences for the last three decades.

This book is designed for those attempting to come to grips with Foucault's voluminous and complex writings. Instead of dealing with them chronologically, however, *A Foucault Primer* concentrates on some of their central concepts, primarily Foucault's rethinking of the categories of discourse, power and the subject (or subjectivity).

'*As an introductory account designed for the non-specialist reader, this book stands out*' Paul Patton, University of Sydney

Framing and Interpretation
GALE MacLACHLAN AND IAN REID

The metaphor of 'framing' is commonly used by those who study socio-cultural texts, and appears to have developed independently in such various disciplines as linguistics, cultural studies, anthropology, psychology, literary criticism, artificial intelligence, aesthetics and the sociology of education. This book is the first to provide a cross-disciplinary exposition and systematic analysis of framing theory and its technical applications. Among the influential theorists of framing whose ideas are critically discussed, special attention is paid to Derrida, Goffman, Bateson, Tannen, Uspensky, Culler, Herrnstein Smith, Schapiro, Bernstein and Minsky.

'*This elegantly written and intriguing book provides an excellent introduction to framing theory*' Ilana Snyder, Monash University

Framing Marginality
Multicultural literary studies
SNEJA GUNEW

What is the status of writings by minority ethnic groups in a country such as Australia, where the literature is in English and the dominant cultural traditions are Anglo-Celtic? How is our understanding of Australian literature affected by that heterogeneous collection of writings described as 'migrant' or 'multicultural'? Sneja Gunew draws on feminist, post-structuralist and post-colonial criticism to examine how non-Anglo-Celtic writings circulate in Australia, and how they are related to comparative multicultural studies, recent critiques of English studies as an imperial apparatus, and the deconstruction of 'universal' notions of culture by such scholars as Said, Bhabha, Spivak and Trinh.

Hypertext
The electronic labyrinth
ILANA SNYDER

Hypertext—a way of connecting text, pictures, film and sound in a non-linear way— is dramatically changing how we read and write, how we teach reading and writing, and how we define literary practices. Ilana Snyder gives a lucid, straightforward overview of the radical effects that hypertext is having on textual practices. Focusing on what we mean by text, author and reader, she explores the connections between the practical experience of hypertext and some of the key insights found in the works of critical theorists such as Barthes and Derrida.

'*a wonderful book . . . pragmatic, direct and clear-eyed scholarship*' Michael Joyce, Vassar College placed in context. *Nuclear Criticism* argues that a broadly based nuclear criticism should be a component of cultural studies in a post-Cold War period characterised by fewer nuclear weapons and more nuclear powers.

'*a most significant addition to an important and criminally under-regarded field*' Frances Bonner, Southern Review

Postmodern Socialism
Romanticism, City and State
PETER BEILHARZ

Injustice, poverty, living and working conditions: the attempt to deal with these social questions arose from a nineteenth-century recognition of the complex problems created mainly in cities. At the same time socialism emerged from a romantic stream of Enlightenment concerned with nature and simplicity. Socialist arguments, now widely viewed as discredited, tackled these problems that ironically remain with us in these postmodern times. By juxtaposing postmodernity and socialism we can generate illuminating perspectives on the way we live *now*. *Postmodern Socialism* traces and criticises these perspectives.

'*an intellectual* tour de force ... *a vital contribution to the debate on* la fin de socialisme' Manfred Steger, Critical Sociology

Reconstructing Theory
Gadamer, Habermas, Luhmann
EDITED BY DAVID ROBERTS

It seems that you cannot be taken seriously in critical thought these days if you are not *au fait* with the works of Foucault, Derrida and other French intellectuals. But there is an alternative tradition for those who find that deconstruction leads only to nihilism and despair.

Reconstructing Theory is an accessible and provocative introduction to the key thinkers of this alternative tradition. It investigates the contributions to social and cultural theory of Gadamer, Habermas and Luhmann, and analyses the influences of Jauss, Iser and Peter and Christa Bürger on literary theory. This book demonstrates that it may after all be possible not only to seek to explain and to criticise the world, but to humanise and even to change it.

Theories of Desire
PATRICK FUERY

Lacan, Barthes, Derrida, Foucault, Kristeva, Cixous, Irigaray: these critical theorists are all linked by their analyses of desire. *Theories of Desire* looks not only at the role of desire in the works of these writers but also examines other major issues and themes of post-structuralism. Fuery considers the place of desire in psychoanalysis, philosophy, literary studies and feminism. He highlights the connections between desire and the critical analysis of subjectivity, language and culture. He investigates the institutionalisation of desire, the relationship between language, discourse and desire, and notes the problems of dealing with women's desire in phallocentric contexts.

Literary Formations
Post-colonialism, nationalism, globalism
ANNE BREWSTER

Literary Formations provides a detailed examination of post-colonial literatures and literary theory. Writing from a feminist perspective, Brewster introduces the issue of gender into a field that has been widely dominated by questions of race and nationalism. She investigates the genre of Aboriginal women's autobiography and looks at the contrasting approaches to nationalism of two 'ethnic' women writers—Bharati Mukherjee in the USA and Ania Walwicz in Australia. Scrutinising the processes of neo-colonisation and the ways in which indigenous, diasporic and multicultural writing are reappropriated by the canon, *Literary Formations* is a valuable introduction to this influential area of critical thinking.

Masculinities and Identities
DAVID BUCHBINDER

Why does masculinity find itself in crisis? This book traces some causes, as well as the developing interest in masculinity and the creation of men's studies, from their origins in feminist and gay political activist theory. David Buchbinder examines the dynamics at work in various cultural constructions of masculinity, not all of which meet with approval in a patriarchal culture. The effects on men of patriarchal ideologies, phallocentrism and male sexuality (both heterosexual and homosexual) are among the issues discussed, while different strands of masculine discourse are identified and examined in a variety of texts ranging from opera to recent news stories.

'a timely, sensible and sensitive book' David Gilbey, Australian Book Review

Metafictions?
Reflexivity in contemporary texts
WENCHE OMMUNDSEN

This book offers an introduction to a literary phenomenon that many find impenetrable or exasperating: 'metafiction', the fiction that is about writing fiction. *Metafictions?* argues that reflexivity is not marginal or derivative but a function central to all literary language. Neither is it a specifically contemporary or postmodern concern, although recent literary theory has increased awareness of the insights reflexivity has to offer on the nature of literary communication. Wenche Ommundsen explains the theoretical framework from which reflexivity is examined and extends the discussion to texts and literatures not generally alluded to in this tradition.

Nuclear Criticism
Ken Ruthven

In the fallout from the obliteration of Hiroshima and Nagasaki was the seed of a new cultural phenomenon: a half-century of writings which attempt to evaluate the cultural consequences of nuclear technology. Ken Ruthven introduces a variety of analytical approaches to representations of nuclearism from official accounts of the first atomic test to recent nuclear controversies. The assumptions and practices of the self-styled, theoretically sophisticated Nuclear Criticism are examined and